BTH 206 25

P9-CEL-580

NO LONGER THE PROPERTY OF
BALDWIN PUBLIC LIBRARY

Getting to
Resolution

Getting to Resolution

Resolution

TURNING CONFLICT INTO

COLLABORATION

STEWART LEVINE

Berrett-Koehler Publishers, Inc.
San Francisco

BALDWIN PUBLIC LIBRARY

Copyright © 1998 by Stewart L. Levine
All rights reserved. No part of this publication may be reproduced, distributed, or transmitted in any form or by any means, including photocopying, recording, or other electronic or mechanical methods, without the prior written permission of the publisher, except in the case of brief quotations embodied in critical reviews and certain other noncommercial uses permitted by copyright law. For permission requests, write to the publisher, addressed "Attention: Permissions Coordinator," at the address below.

Berrett-Koehler Publishers, Inc.
450 Sansome Street, Suite 1200
San Francisco, CA 94111-3320
Tel: 415-288-0260   Fax: 415-362-2512

Ordering information
Individual sales. Berrett-Koehler publications are available through most bookstores. They can also be ordered direct from Berrett-Koehler at the address above.

Quantity sales. Special discounts are available on quantity purchases by corporations, associations, and others. For details, write to the "Special Sales Department" at the Berrett-Koehler address above.

Orders for college textbook/course adoption use. Please contact Berrett-Koehler Publishers at the address above.

Orders by U.S. trade bookstores and wholesalers. Please contact Publishers Group West, 4065 Hollis St., Box 8843, Emeryville, CA 94608; 510-658-3453; 1-800-788-3123.

Printed in the United States of America

Printed on acid-free and recycled paper that is composed of 50% recovered fiber, including 10% postconsumer waste.

Library of Congress Cataloging-in-Publication Data
Levine, Stewart.
    Getting to resolution : turning conflict into collaboration / Stewart Levine.
        p.   cm.
    Includes bibliographical references and index.
    ISBN 1-57675-005-1 (alk. paper)
        1. Dispute resolution (Law)—United States.   2. Mediation—United States.
    3. Conflict management.   I. Title.
KF9084.L48   1998
347.73′9—dc21   97-47473
                                                                                                            CIP

First printing: January 1998
01 00 99 98   10 9 8 7 6 5 4 3 2 1

For Adeline & Meyer

Imagine all the people living life in peace.
You can say I'm a dreamer, but I'm not the only one.
I hope some day you'll join us.
And the world will be as ONE.

—*John Lennon,* Imagine

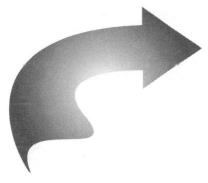

Contents

Part III

New Thinking That Fosters
Resolution: Ten Principles   **43**

Part IV

The Resolution Model in Practice:
A Step-by-Step Guide   **95**

Lists and Charts

Preface

During my second year of law school I had my first "real" lawyer's job. I was an intern at a local legal services clinic. On my first day I was handed 25 cases "to work on." This would be my job for the semester. Three weeks later I asked the managing attorney for more cases. When he asked about the 25 he had given me, I told him that I had resolved them.

He was very surprised—and very curious. He asked how I had done it. I told him that I had reviewed the files, spoken to the clients, thought about a fair outcome and what needed to be done, called the attorney or agency on the other side, and reached a satisfactory resolution.

I knew nothing about being a lawyer. I had no inclination that the cases were difficult, needed to take a long time, or had to be handled in any particular way. With common sense and a "beginner's mind," I found the solution that worked best for all concerned. Simple? It was for me!

I spent the next 12 years becoming a "successful" lawyer—and becoming less effective at resolving matters. Then, feeling frustrated, anxious, and fearful, I stopped practicing law. I have spent the last 15 years recovering what I knew about resolution when I started, discovering its component parts and learning how to teach and model it for others.

As a young attorney, although I listened politely to more senior lawyers, I was surprised at the coaching I received. Standard practice discouraged communication among the parties in conflict, communication that I had used in my legal services cases, communication essential for efficient resolution. Many lawyers were playing a very different game from the one my natural instincts chose.

Yet, I was fascinated with how the most effective judges and lawyers understood people's real concerns. They knew what to honor and what to respect. They knew how to frame situations and condition people's expectations. They embodied a tradition that accommodated competing concerns and built consensus. Winning or losing was not the point of their work. Their game was resolution and getting people back to their lives.

I had a similar orientation, and this orientation coupled with my belief that everyone had a lot to learn about conflict, focused me on trying to understand conflict, this pervasive aspect of life. Amid all the business and personal conflict, there was some clarity: we could do a lot better at managing conflict, and we could prevent conflict if we formed new business and personal relationships in a different way.

I am motivated to use resources most efficiently and to minimize the emotional fallout from conflict. That drives me; that catalyzes resolution. This book shares what I have learned from observation, study, and reflection. That journey continues.

My Objectives

I have specific goals for this book:

> 1. Change your thinking about conflict. By providing a new set of principles and values, I would like you to shift from thinking about problems, fighting, and breakdowns to think-

ing about engagement, learning, creativity, and the opportunity for creating value.

2. Provide a model for resolution. This model consists of specific, tangible steps for you to follow when conflict is present in any situation or when you start new professional or personal relationships.

3. Inspire you to develop a new perspective toward conflict. With this new perspective you could avoid the emotional hassle, the cost of unproductive energy, and the waste of resources. You would know that no matter how hopeless it seems, no matter how strong the emotional impulse to fight and win, resolution could be discovered within any situation.

4. Steward a mind-set of resolution. I want to teach you a model that fosters dignity and integrity; optimizes your resources; and allows all concerns to be voiced, honored, and woven into the resolution.

5. Foster a culture based on principles and practices of resolution and agreement. I hope the book motivates you to become a "resolutionary" in your life and a leader of others in practicing resolution, while at the same time appreciating the richness that the creative tension of differences provides.

6. Enable you to take personal responsibility for dealing with conflict, diversity, and disagreement.

This last goal is critical. We are living at a time of great crisis, as well as great opportunity. We can thrive *if* we design a world order that provides stability, optimizes natural resources, preserves the environment, controls population, and shifts our thinking from rights and entitlements to service and responsibility. This process starts with each individual. You must tend your own garden. As a first step I encourage you to develop a spirit of resolution. Given our "shrinking planet" and the increasing transactions of our global village, learning to take responsibility for effective collaborations and resolving the inevitable conflicts is essential.

Now is the time to start working together more effectively!

The Contents

This book is based on four simple premises:

1. Conflict is expensive.

2. Efficient conflict resolution requires a new paradigm of collaboration grounded on ten principles (delineated in Part II).

3. Efficient conflict resolution requires using a new systematic approach—a model that is applied consistently and that reinforces the new paradigm through routine use.

4. The resolution of conflict using the model returns you to productive lives and functional relationships.

Part I of the book sets out its context. Chapter 1 explains what resolution is and why it is so valuable. Chapter 2 details the ways that conflict is expensive—the great individual and collective cost we incur on a daily basis as we work within the standard ways of handling conflict. I list, illustrate, and explain the cost of conflict so you can appreciate the huge expense. You see that under current practices, "winners" are losing. This fact is important because capitalist culture is based on economics and profit. I hope recognition of all the costs will motivate you to use the new practices.

Part II shares a case study that introduces the model for resolution (Chapter 3) and gives an overview of the steps in the model (Chapter 4).

Part III explains the new principles (new thinking) for resolving conflict. Current practices of the old paradigm are based on an underlying set of beliefs, beliefs that may have served you in a world based on power and control. That world, I sense, is fading, and it's time to adjust your thinking. The new principles reflect current, more enlightened thought. These principles are the foundation for new practices of the resolution model.

Part IV provides a more detailed explanation of the resolution model introduced in Part II. Part IV also demonstrates the model in action, embodying the values of the new principles. It shares some of the results that have been achieved by following the model.

Part V addresses how the new resolution principles and model fit within current standard ways of resolving conflict. It also introduces the experts available to help you use the new principles and model—what they do and how to choose one.

Part VI provides a peek into what it can be like if you follow the principles and practices of resolution.

How This Book Will Help You

The book is written for many groups. Everyone looking for a way to reduce the stress involved in collaborating with others, personally and in business, will find value. People who work with and for others will learn how to structure their employment relationships.

For executives, managers, human resource and training personnel, business owners, and employees who must do more with less, this book will help increase productivity and improve communication and coordination among intercompany and intracompany teams.

Entrepreneurs and business developers who must build "virtual organizations" will find this book useful. For consultants, lawyers, architects, and accountants (whose business depends on satisfied clients), this book will provide tools for clearly articulating expectations and constructing sound business relationships at the beginning of those relationships. For managers, executives, mediators, lawyers, and psychologists (the increasing cadre working in the field of conflict resolution), this book provides new tools and insights.

People who desire social change will embrace the new paradigm. Individuals seeking formulas for more effective use of societal resources will value the way resources can be conserved. Folks who bristle at litigiousness will see that the number of lawsuits can be reduced if we adopt the new principles as primary values.

Consumers of legal services, and those who are afraid of legal services, will see potential for huge financial and emotional savings. People looking for a professional who will enter into a more heartfelt relationship based on a shared covenant will learn to identify such professionals and the standards that can be used to formulate a satis-factory and predictable service-based relationship.

Married people, family members, and those in other partnerships can construct agreements to guide them to deeper connection, under-standing, and less stressful relationships.

Beginner's Mind

Please take on the dignity of a "beginner's mind" as you try the new practices. Be patient with yourself during the learning process. Most of you want to be experts immediately. You want to conquer the ex-pert slopes on the mountain, master the new software, or take off on your new roller blades with little practice. Cut yourself some slack in gaining comfort and competence with the new practices. I guarantee it will be worth it.

Following the principles and the model will enhance the quality of your life, the lives of those around you, and the communities you are part of. The principles embody values that we all want to embrace. The model is simple, but applying it is challenging. Using new practices and developing new habits requires mindfulness, commitment, and repetition. As you acquire competence, you will become artful and able to discern how much formal attention to the steps in the model some situations require, and what steps are not necessary in other sit-uations. At the beginning I suggest that you practice using every step. That will help you internalize all the principles and practices.

Acknowledgments

Inspiration for this book came from many sources. Gus Lee, the au-thor of *China Boy*, was critical. As director of the Office of Education of the State Bar of California, he reviewed a script I wrote for a medi-ation video and said, "You have a very important message to deliver to the public. I want you to write a book."

From my parents, Adeline and Meyer, I learned about values, ethics, and integrity. They admonished me to find what I loved, and success would follow. Susan Howard taught me to believe I was capable of accomplishing anything I wanted. John Haynes demonstrated the mood and process of mediation. I learned about leadership and resolution—my best work—from Marsha Shenk, who helped uncover the idea of "agreements for results." Bud Seith personified male mothering. Marty Africa is a daily demonstration of courage, perseverance, responsibility, and commitment; I thank her for shelter in the storm. From my brothers Peter, Bill, Larry, Cliff, and Steve I learned the joy of camaraderie. My sister Sharron has taught me about acceptance. I thank Tish for her joy. I thank David for being there, and for the example that he is.

I thank Steve Piersanti, the founder of Berrett-Koehler, for recognizing the value of this project. His vision and nurturing of my ideas was extraordinary. Laurie Harper of the Sebastian Agency falls in that category. I thank the readers who reviewed the manuscript for their thoughtful comments, especially Charlie Dorris and Barbara Kimmel for their careful editing and Detta Penna for her artful design work. I thank my clients and the students at all of my courses for their contributions to this body of work, and I thank the entire Berrett-Koehler staff for getting it out.

Most of all I acknowledge you, the reader. Thank you for your "resolve" to grow and to make your life, and the lives of those around you, more peaceful.

Stewart Levine
January 1998

Part I

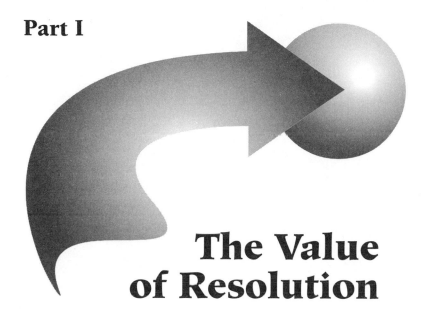

The Value
of Resolution

Part I provides a context for the book.
This section reveals all the costs of conflict
and shows how the current system
for resolving conflict
actually breeds more conflict.
These chapters define resolution
and demonstrate how
resolution provides value.

Chapter One

Resolution: Getting Beyond Conflict, Compromise, and Settlement

Through dialogue, even the most unresolvable conflicts can be worked out and everyone wins. The process did not include litigation or the emotional roller coaster ride that accompanies most conflicts. It was a delightful experience.

—Bill Brown, president, Influence Communications

Settlement of a lawsuit is often characterized by thinking that "if both sides are unhappy, you probably have a good settlement." Resolution is much better than settling! Resolution provides relief and completeness. The situation no longer gnaws at your gut.

The most fitting dictionary definitions of *resolution* are: (1) the act of unraveling a perplexing question or problem; (2) solution; and (3) removal or disappearance, as the disappearance of a tumor.

The last is the most important. It means "as if it never happened." The gnawing effect that I call *internal chatter* has disappeared. The lack of chatter frees you to focus energy and attention on the present. If you've ever had a back injury, poison ivy, or broken a bone, you

Chapter opening quotes, unless otherwise referenced, are from *The Forbes Scrapbook of Thoughts on the Business of Life*, New York: B.C. Forbes & Son, 1950.

know what I mean. Something is resolved when the injury or illness does not impede your present moment's activities.

This is important. You don't want to keep dealing with the current impact of yesterday's conflict. The effect may consist of holding anger or resentment, or thinking the result or compromise was unfair. Perhaps you compromised to get the situation behind you, or you deferred to someone else's decision.

For over 25 years as a lawyer, mediator, consultant, and trainer I have practiced a "resolutionary"[1] attitude. Looking for the fair outcome from everyone's perspective leads to resolution. Whether you are a hired advocate or have a personal stake in the situation, you can adopt an "attitude of resolution." In this way you become an "observer" of what might be fair in the situation, even though you are directly involved. Developing the attitude of resolution is a skill you can cultivate. I have found this orientation far more effective than trying to "win."

Why Resolution

Have you ever met someone who could not stop talking about what happened in the past? These people constantly reference the event. It pervades their life as if it happened yesterday, although it took place 20 years ago. They are stuck in the past, cut off from the ability to fully participate in their life.

Conflict has an emotional cost that remains after the battle is over. Win or lose, the scars may be with you for the rest of your life. People spend their lives focusing on the promotion they "lost," the business they "lost," the divorce they "lost," the project they "lost." This tunnel vision keeps them gripped, locked in their own anger.

Even if they won, they may not have healed the real cause of the conflict—a breakdown in a relationship that was valuable enough for them to invest emotional energy in a battle. They never completed grieving, and they still carry the emotional suffering. They never "resolved" the real issue. They may even have never identified it! Our current systems and ways of thinking (winning) guarantee a cost—suffering. The small battles between partners, parents and children, and employees and bosses take a significant toll.

Productivity and satisfaction, in business and personal relationships, come from our ability to collaborate with others. When you are resolved, you can fully focus on the tasks at hand. Your efforts are undiluted. Unresolved conflict, on the other hand, is an impediment to productivity and to satisfying, functional relationships. In today's world of "knowledge work," focus and creativity are essential. It's impossible to be fully productive when you are angry. That's why getting resolved about the situation that's sapping your strength and attention is very important.

It's equally important to have a sense of resolution when you start any new relationship. You collaborate with others by reaching agreements. Sometimes these agreements are explicit, often they are implicit. If you look at your activities through a "lens" of agreement, you can see that your dependence on others is based on an intricate, pervasive web of implicit and explicit agreements. When you start out with uncertainty or come into conflict during a project, you recognize some of the cost of not being resolved. You also realize how inadequate your agreement-making and conflict-resolution tools are. Even though making agreements and resolving conflicts are core skills for working with others, these skills are not taught to most of us.

Our current paradigm for resolving conflicts and starting collaborative relationships hinders us because of the way we were programmed to think and because of the standard systems and practices in place. This book provides you with the following new tools:

1. Ten principles of a new paradigm—a new way of thinking about conflict resolution.

2. A seven-step model for resolving conflict—a road map of new behaviors. These principles and this model will maximize your ability to resolve conflict and achieve desired results in any business or personal relationship.

The Key Challenge

The primary hurdle in getting to resolution is reaching an *agreement in principle*—a broad understanding of what the resolution will be. Once you have an agreement in principle, filling in the details is not difficult. You get to an agreement in principle by crossing an emotional barrier: you let go of the position you have taken. For most people, this is not easy. It requires going against a lifetime of dealing with conflict in a different way. The steps of the model are designed to get you over this hurdle.

Getting beyond the emotional barrier is not like personal therapy. The internal work is accomplished as a result of new thinking—adopting the values of the ten principles of the new paradigm—and new actions—following the steps of the model. Every step of the model contributes to resolution by making you speak your thoughts, feelings, and perceptions about the conflict. Once your position is articulated and no longer purely emotional, you and others can deal with it.

Although the steps of the model seem linear, getting to resolution is not a linear process. Mechanically going through the steps will not lead to resolution unless you have embraced the values of the ten principles. Once you embrace the principles, you will have achieved the model's first step, called the Attitude of Resolution. Then, each successive step takes you toward resolution by making you go deeper into the personal, emotional, and human aspects of the conflict. You don't have to say "yes" to the principles because they feel good, seem right, or are morally or politically correct. It's fine to buy in because the cost of remaining in the conflict is too great. What is important is to get into the personal, emotional, and human aspects of the conflict; regardless of what you say the conflict is about, the conflict is between you and at least one other person.

The new model contains a systematic approach. When you learn something new, it is important to have standard practices to follow. Standards provide guidance as you learn the new skill. When you learn to ski, drive a car, or fly an airplane, you put in place fundamentals that become unconscious habits. The model provides these fundamentals. Using the model develops habit and competence, and you discover the value of the principles. When you gain competence you will start to develop your own "artistry"—innovations within the standard practices. Once you internalize the principles and steps, resolution can happen very quickly!

The Value of Resolution at Work

As organizations cut costs, differentiate products, and streamline productivity, people need to work within increasingly complex webs of collaboration toward common goals. They need tools that foster collaboration in the face of conflict. Rather than staying angry and stuck, you must learn skills that foster resolution and return you to productivity. This book provides the model for the conversations among people that result in the collaborations essential for getting more done with fewer resources. This book reveals how "agreement"—the final step of resolving a conflict or the first step in the beginning of a new relationship—is an ongoing process, and that conflict and diverse opinions are opportunities for creativity and innovation. You will learn how to establish agreements based on deep heartfelt connection—agreements based on covenant.

Some of the benefits of establishing agreements based on covenant include:

Establishing shared vision of senior management

Improving teamwork

Creating partnership

Motivating participation

Including diverse perspectives and opinions

Using differences productively

Coordinating with external teammates

Using resources efficiently

Communicating more effectively

Building self-managing, high performance teams

Forging consensus quickly

Fostering an environment of learning and growth

Promoting continuous improvement

Capitalizing on the advantages of virtual organizations

This book gives organizations, individuals, and managers the tools to achieve these benefits.

The Value of Resolution at Home

Besides its applications in business and workplace settings, the tools in the book will unlock more satisfying and intimate personal relationships within marriages, families, and less traditional partnerships that are part of our diverse, emerging social fabric. Because we think about personal relationships from an emotional and romantic perspective, it is difficult to accept that a process for resolving conflict and constructing agreements with specific promises about behavior will be helpful in producing more satisfying intimate relationships. My experience tells me otherwise.

Personal Responsibility for the Value of Resolution

Most of us avoid taking personal responsibility for conflict resolution. Although litigious, we often lack the courage to deeply connect with others. We personally avoid confrontation. If we have a disagreement in a business transaction or with a neighbor, we may let a lawyer take care of it. If we have emotional conflict, we may visit a therapist or counselor who we hope will tell us what to do.

Conflict is usually recognized by pain and discomfort. When you take personal responsibility, you get to the root of the pain much faster than if you ask someone else to resolve the situation for you. This requires being vulnerable. If you are unwilling or unable to be authentic about your feelings, you may be quick to give up responsibility, and instead take false safety and security behind a more sterile, professional process. In doing that, you give up the possibility of discovering your real concerns, getting to the core of the conflict, and reaching resolution.

Delegating conflict resolution to third-party professionals who know how to diagnose and resolve our problems is a culturally learned response. Delegation, however, compromises us because the professionals are trained to believe—and do believe—that they are better equipped than we are to make key decisions that affect the core of our lives. These conflicts are filled with our feelings and emotions, and the professional we hand the conflict to does not have to live with the resolution.

This book is a call for personal responsibility. It asks you to adopt new practices, and to assume a new attitude in the world. It requests that you take personal responsibility for dealing with conflict, diversity and disagreement—that you become "ResponseAble." Giving the process away deprives you of the satisfaction of "getting to resolution." When you are involved you are uniquely capable of designing the best resolution. You derive value, strength, and the sense of self that full participation provides. Of course, there will be times when you need help. This book is designed to provide the guidance you may need.

Learning New Behaviors

This book is a learning tool. My overriding concern is that you learn new behaviors: new practices that will improve your professional and personal life. If you keep doing the same thing, you will keep getting the same results. An insane person gets upset at having the same outcomes, even though the person persists in the same behavior. Learning is the ability to take new actions so you achieve new results. Unless you implement new behaviors, you have not learned anything.

This book will not be hard to understand. Your life experience has taught you many of the skills you need to master the art of resolution. The challenge is implementation—developing the habit of living the principles on a daily basis.

As background research for the book, I spoke with over 100 senior conflict resolution professionals. Their insights validated many of the ideas in the book. The stories in the book are true, although some of them are composites. They have been disguised to cloak the identity of individuals and organizations. The book contains illustrations in which I served as a facilitator, but the principles and processes are just as valuable in situations in which you are personally involved. You can be both facilitator and participant by internalizing the model and learning to become an "observer" of your personal circumstances. It's a goal of the book. You want to become "meta" to the situation, which means to be outside or above it. I do it all the time, and you can too. The resolution principles and model can also be used for third-party interventions—when you try to help friends or co-workers resolve a conflict in which you are not personally involved, or as manager when you have direct responsibility.

I am inspired by the paradigm of resolution. I hope to inspire you. *Getting to Resolution* will teach you about patience, inquiry, learning, and expanding your perspective. The power and integrity of resolution leads to outcomes you cannot invent yourself. It's the difference between the sound of one hand clapping and two!

Getting to Resolution helps you understand what you already know about conflict. It shows you a simpler, more effective approach to reaching, modifying, and maintaining agreement, a key to your professional and personal success.

Summary

Resolution is taking care of conflict so that there are no lingering aftereffects. It is better than compromising because the cost of the aftereffects is less. The key challenge is reaching agreements in principle. This becomes easier when we adopt the values of the ten principles of the new paradigm and engage in the dialogues that the resolution model prescribes. Resolution has great value at work, at home, and within yourself. It is a skill you can learn by developing the habit of the new practices.

Reflections

Please take a few minutes and reflect about your attitude toward conflict. Think about your early environment and how conflict was handled. Have you adopted, without consciously choosing, the patterns you saw as a child? Do those patterns serve you? How do the ways you handle conflict make difficult situations worse? What would it be like if you could behave in ways that lead to the results you really wanted? How might your life be different?

Chapter Two

The Many Costs of Conflict

I appreciate being able to handle this matter without investing any more time, effort and money than was necessary.

—Karl Bareither, president, Family Business Consultants

In 1994, 18 million cases were filed in U.S. courts at a cost of $300 billion.[2] I once read that 20% of Fortune 500 senior executives' time is spent in litigation-related activities. Imagine the tally that adds up to. It's commonplace for legal fees to exceed the value of the amount at stake. Years ago, if a situation had more than $100,000 at stake, litigation was a viable alternative. Today the benchmark is $1 million and growing quickly. Following the old paradigm is very costly!

The cost of conflict represents a resource drain of huge proportion and a source of great unhappiness and discomfort.

Why So Expensive?

Traditional court systems, what you may think of as the usual way of resolving conflicts, do not foster resolution. Their operative premise is that someone will win. Our dispute resolution machinery often fuels the fire of conflict and impedes resolution. Worse, while engaged in the conflict resolution process, your productive activity, what your life is really about, is diluted. The system does not foster resolutions that address the underlying sources of conflict—breakdowns in relationship. The process is not designed to get people back to an optimal state of productivity.

The current system embodies struggle, control, and a survival of the fittest mentality. It is based on dialectic, right/wrong, either/or patterns that originated in Aristotelian logic. Even though we live in a densely populated, rapidly changing technological world that cries out for systems that foster collaboration, individuals and institutions tenaciously cling to old habits.

Elected representatives, mostly lawyers, to whom we have abdicated control, sometimes believe that we can legislate ways of treating each other. Often they have a knee-jerk response to enact a new rule or regulation in response to a problem. This does not work. The standards essential for a functional social fabric cannot be legislated. What's missing are the bedrock ethics and values that were taught by the educational community and religious institutions and were fostered in extended families. These values have become clouded in our modern, mobile, sound-bite techno-society.

Because family structures and religious institutions have become so fragmented, we no longer rely on them to provide the education of core values. Many people seek external standards that will tell them what to do. People often have little grounding in collaborative skills because real partnership flows from within the "covenantal" relationships that community, family, and religious institutions have traditionally demanded and fostered. Many people have no role models and sadly, in many instances, don't know how to treat each other from within a common covenant.

In a recent interview, noted futurist Alvin Toffler, author of *Future Shock, The Third Wave,* and *Powershift,* stated: "The place we need really imaginative new ideas is in conflict theory. That's true with respect to war and peace, but also it's true domestically. The real weakness throughout the country is the lack of conflict resolution methods other than litigation and guns."[3]

Toffler is on the right track. Our current crisis is caused by both the aspects of today's conflict resolution system and the way that it is administered, such as:

- Increase in the body of statuary and case law reflecting the growing numbers of lawyers, and complex transactions requiring regulation.

- Commercialization of the legal tradition fostered by competition and advertising.

- Growing reliance on counselors and therapists who care for our internal conflict and feed our conflict-avoidance mentality.

- Breakdown of trust and the inability to assess the value of, or need for, specific actions that therapists or lawyers take (evidenced by growing malpractice claims).

- Attorneys' conflict of interest because their practice of hourly billing results in a devotion to process, not results.

- The growth of the contingent fee and a class of cases in which there is nothing to lose by taking a chance.

- The legal, economic, and emotional minefields of the litigation process.

- The myth of finding truth and justice in a courtroom, a myth that has been perpetuated by the role models celebrated on TV.

These reasons are symptoms. They evidence a breakdown in the covenants of trust between people who are members of the same "community." They point to a lack of communication. People are focusing on themselves. They are concerned about their "rights" and "entitlements" without thinking about their *responsibilities* toward others. This all flows from the win/lose systems and practices that are in place.

Many people are looking for guideposts and rules that will tell them how to treat each other. This requires new practices and new ways of thinking, which are the subject of this book. Before discussing them, let's examine the cost of doing things the present way. As we review the many different costs, imagine how much more you might accomplish if you could harness the resources expended, the money and energy used in the battle of traditional conflict resolution. Imagine using those resources to produce the outcomes you want.

The Cost of Conflict

The cost of conflict is composed of the following:

1. *Direct Cost*	Fees of lawyers and other professionals
2. *Productivity Cost*	Value of lost time The opportunity cost of what those involved would otherwise be producing
3. *Continuity Cost*	Loss of ongoing relationships including the "community" they embody
4. *Emotional Cost*	The pain of focusing on and being held hostage by our emotions

It's important to identify the costs of our current paradigm and examine some tangible examples. Recognizing the cost, I hope, will motivate change.

Direct Costs

Because of an inability to face conflicts, many of you spend money you can't afford on professional gladiators hired to do your bidding. A divorce between two people whose only asset is their home can transform that residence into legal fees. The process brings out the worst in people who thought enough of each other to marry, but now can't even sit down and talk.

An Empty Victory. The Cobbs were involved in a lawsuit about water run-off and erosion problems that had not been disclosed to them when they purchased a new home from a professional relocation company. What started as their claim for $30,000 to repair water damage and reroute a driveway resulted in a four-year battle with legal fees of over $175,000 and engineering experts' fees of $25,000.

As the situation escalated, the Cobbs realized they had invested so much in professional fees they couldn't afford to lose their suit. They had to continue the fight. Mrs. Cobb was increasingly agitated because her husband had pushed the battle forward. The relocation company became more resolute in wanting to prove it was right. The company tied up the energy of its in-house counsel, two lawyers from a litigation firm, a senior company executive, and a real estate broker. All of this energy was focused on something that had happened four years earlier in which no one had intentionally done anything to harm anyone else. The end result was an empty victory. The Cobbs won, but the judge did not award them attorney fees—their only hope of getting even financially because the actual cost to repair the loss was only $30,000.

Sally and Frank. Sally and Frank were married for over 20 years. While she was not committed to a divorce, Sally was clear that she could no longer tolerate things as they were. Sally finally mustered the courage to tell Frank what she was thinking and her vision of the changes needed if the marriage was to continue. Frank became immovable. Sally and her closest friends tried to convince Frank that it was best for them to separate; maybe, during a cooling-off period with some distance between them, they could create a new foundation for their relationship. Frank could not hear the advice of his peers, professionals, or his family.

After many unanswered requests for Frank to sit down and work out a solution, Sally filed for divorce. Frank dug in his heels. He cut off financial support. Although Frank was advised that to get the reconciliation he wanted he was better off leaving for a while, he chose to engage in a battle that could have no winners. Frank hired an attorney who mirrored his own attitude. They would not pay one dime or cooperate until ordered by a judge.

Sally and Frank ran up tens of thousands of dollars in lawyers' fees. Thousands were spent on psychological evaluations by therapists and by accountants who valued Frank's business. Each side had their own experts, as well as those appointed by the court.

Although part of the current paradigm, these fees are a waste of resources. The amount would have been better spent on setting up new households for Frank and Sally. The experts' fees could have been devoted to building self-esteem in the present and counseling for the transition. Instead, they were devoted to an already dead past. For Sally and Frank, a simple process at the outset would have made the situation history.

Productivity Cost

Time is a valuable, limited commodity. When people are focused on rehashing the past, they cannot create and produce value in the present. There are two aspects of this cost—direct loss and opportunity cost. The direct loss is the value of a person's time—what the person should be earning but is not being paid because he or she engaged in the conflict. The opportunity cost is the value the person might have produced if his or her energy was focused on creation and innovation.

Intellectual Property. Two colleagues designed two innovative forms of management "technology." These processes were significant additions to the knowledge base about personal productivity and leadership. They battled for over a year about who owned the intellectual property they had developed. The productivity loss from their feud boggles the mind. Instead of many students and clients getting the value of what they discovered, their time was devoted to fighting. That direct loss was their loss in revenue. The opportunity cost consisted of the value of new innovations that might have been developed during the conflict. (Another loss is the value each student might have produced.)

Sally and Frank—Part 2. In Sally and Frank's situation, Frank was focused on the conflict, not on his business; his capacity was diminished during the entire conflict because of his mental preoccupation. For example, if he earned $2,000 per week, he was completely out of work for six weeks of court time, and his capacity was diminished by 25% for the two-year period of litigation, the direct productivity loss would be $64,000.

$$\$2{,}000 \times 6 \text{ weeks} = \$12{,}000$$
$$\underline{\$2{,}000 \text{ per week} \times 104 \text{ weeks} \times 25\% = \$52{,}000}$$
$$\$64{,}000$$

The opportunity cost is harder to calculate, but probably Frank's attention to the divorce caused him to miss opportunities such as designing new profit centers for his business, capitalizing on special sales of merchandise, or expanding his operations.

Continuity Cost

Continuity costs result from being stuck in the past—costs such as the loss of relationship and community.

Lifelong Friends. Mira and Angela were like sisters. They had grown up together and had married and raised children at the same time. They lived in the same community. They were enriched by the strength of their relationship. Hardly a day went by that they did not spend time together. Their connection was a lifeline, a great blessing for both of them. When their children entered high school, they decided it was time to go into business together.

They were children of the '60s who had always sparked each other's creativity. Their lives had never been about accumulating wealth; they just wanted to hang out together. They opened a casual store—clothing, housewares, novelties. It was a modern-day general store staffed by pleasant people. The mood of the shop was a respite from the cold experience of many retail establishments.

They were an instant hit. The store grew. They added a cafe. They opened a second and a third store. Eight years later there were 23 outlets, and Mira and Angela were making more money than they dreamed possible. They got to spend most days together and were very happy. What a life! Their husbands and children joined the business. They were building a solid foundation.

Years before, Mira and Angela had pledged never to let money or possessions come between them. Unfortunately, their husbands had not taken the same vow. Mira's husband Alberto had worked in the financial services industry. The idea of taking the company public put dollar signs in his eyes. His early investigation revealed that Mira and Angela could each pocket $6 million by selling 40% of the company stock. Angela wanted nothing to do with investment bankers and the close scrutiny that federal regulators would bring. She was very concerned about losing the flavor of what had made them successful. But Alberto was hungry . . . aggressive . . . and greedy!

Greed can do amazing things to people. Alberto started to undermine the Mira-Angela team. He created a crack that turned into a huge chasm. Ramon, Angela's husband, tried to open a dialogue, but Alberto was too headstrong. He was intent on proving he was right, that not taking the company public would lead to its downfall. The mood that had made the company successful was lost. The spark was fading. Profits were falling. Angela stopped talking to Mira because she couldn't control Alberto. One after another, the stores were closed. Angela and Mira were alone. They never spoke again.

Three Feet of Real Estate. Joanne asked me to represent her in a lawsuit filed by her next door neighbor. For over 30 years Joanne had treated a three-foot strip of property adjacent to her driveway as if she owned it. Joanne planted flowers and maintained the lawn. On a visual inspection it was obvious that the property belonged to her. One day, however, her neighbor Ruth required a survey as part of a refinancing. The survey revealed that technically the strip was owned by Ruth.

Because the relationship was cordial, I was surprised that no informal demand or letter had been sent by Ruth before the lawsuit. I reviewed the documents and replied to the suit. I suggested that Joanne meet with Ruth to discuss the situation. She agreed, but to Joanne's surprise Ruth refused to speak about the situation. Her attorney took a similar posture with me. I believed Joanne had an 80% chance of prevailing if we went to court because her long-term use of the land had never been protested. I told Joanne, however, that there was always risk in going to court and it would be wise to make a settlement offer. She agreed to do that. The other side refused to negotiate. We did go to court. The judge suggested a settlement. Again no response from Ruth. We won, but it was an empty victory.

Joanne found out that Ruth was acting on the advice of her attorney, including the refusal to communicate. Joanne could not let go of her anger. She felt like a criminal, even though she never had any evil intent and she had won the lawsuit. Two years later Joanne sold the home she loved. She could no longer stand the anger she felt whenever she looked at the strip of land.

Brother and Sister. Seth and Sarah had a bitter fight over their father's estate. Growing up, they had been close confidants. And even though distance grew between them because of a geographical separation, they remained devoted to each other. When their father died, however, they had a disagreement about family money that had been given to Seth to invest in a business. Was that money a gift or an advance on his inheritance? They were both partly correct in their positions and were both convinced they could win in court. They both lost the war. Seth and Sarah did not speak for 30 years. At the funeral of their brother Steve, they looked at each other and broke down in tears, knowing they could never regain what they had lost.

Emotional Cost

Sometimes there are situations you can't let go of: a fight with a spouse, boss, co-worker, neighbor, friend, partner, or the person who ran into your car. The emotions of anger, fear, and blame grip you and force a reaction that saps your current productive capacity. Instead of going about your business, you are riveted on the injustice done to you and the untoward behavior of the perpetrator. You are consumed with vengeance and desire to punish the wrongdoer. You expend energy on your anger in addition to the loss you already have suffered. All of this energy will never be recovered.

The Revenge of the Past. Randy finally received the promotion he was longing for. That was the good news. The bad news was his inability to focus on his job. He was going through a messy child custody battle with his ex-wife. That stirred up all of the anger he was holding about the past relationship. She wanted to mediate the dispute, but Randy was set on winning. Unfortunately he lost—his job. It was a position that required all of his attention. He missed two important deadlines because his mind was focused on the past.

Sally and Frank—Part 3. Sally and Frank remained embroiled in legal turmoil for almost two years. Sally had to go to court for every ounce of relief: to get Frank out of their marital home, to force him to provide basic support, and to get him to pay the mortgage. She won each little skirmish, but Sally and Frank, and their children, have suffered huge amounts of emotional trauma. Sally and Frank hardly speak to each other; their children are having very difficult teenage years; their respective parents, previously social friends, do not speak to each other; and they were paralyzed in getting on with their lives. They will never be the same.

Major life changes are never easy, but doing legal battle over issues that are essentially emotional is like playing baseball on an ice hockey rink. For the balance of their lives, Sally and Frank will suffer because they would not let go of the past. They will never be friends. Their children are scarred. You can't put a price tag on these emotional losses, but the cost is huge. What might have been a simple process turned into a situation in which the conflicts escalated and the pain, suffering, and scars are magnified.

Summary

Current attitudes and systems of conflict resolution foster conflict. Conflict is very expensive. It consists of the following, never to be recovered, costs: (1) direct cost—professional fees; (2) opportunity cost—what would otherwise be produced; (3) continuity cost—the loss of relationships and "community"; (4) emotional cost—the pain of being held prisoner by emotions.

Reflections

Think about the "expensive" conflicts in your own life. What was the direct cost? The cost of professionals? The opportunity cost? The emotional cost? The relationship cost? As you reflect on your situation, think about the different actions and results you might have had if you had taken a different tack. How might you do it differently next time? How would your life be different?

Part II

A
Better Way of
Resolving Conflict

If resolution is so good,
how do you get there,
and what does it look like?
Part II provides an introduction
to the steps of the model of resolution
and a case study of a
successful application.

Chapter Three

Two Brothers: A Story of Resolution

> *I saw little hope in coming to a fair settlement. . . . [E]ach of the others I had gotten advice from led me to believe the only solution was a court battle. . . . I found the resolution model representative of the concerns of a partner. . . . [W]e each walked away with a feeling of winning.*
>
> —Bill Thomas, president, Integrated Promotions

Sometimes new ways of doing things are not readily understood. They do not fit with the way our perceptual systems have been conditioned. We cannot see what we are not already expecting.

A classic illustration is the story about the watchmaking industry. BQ—Before Quartz—the Swiss held about 95% of the market. In the early 1960s the Swiss R & D people presented their innovation, the quartz movement, to the barons of the industry. The barons could not perceive the innovation. It did not have a mainspring, moving parts, or jewels. It could not possibly be a timepiece. The Japanese saw it, and the rest is history.[4] You may have a similar response to the paradigm of this book. I want to give you a look at the big picture first.

Just as a picture is worth a thousand words, a good story is worth pages of explanation. I hope that the following story showing the

principles and model in action brings the new paradigm alive and motivates you to embrace it.

The Story of Two Brothers

Two brothers were running a family enterprise that their grandfather
had started. The business was profitable, was well located, and had a
fine reputation. Their city was growing, and the economy was expanding. Life was good. The brothers each married and began to raise
families.

Tom, the younger brother, wanted to expand the business. He
hired a consultant and then approached his brother Bill and asked
him to be his partner in growing the family enterprise. Trusting and
open-minded, Bill listened carefully to his brother's ideas and to those
of the consultant. He studied the situation with them. After consider-
able reflection and some hesitancy, he agreed to support the new direction. There was a family legacy of integrity to uphold, and Bill was
concerned about his brother's motives.

The consultant recommended hiring new people. One was an ambitious young man. Bill was not comfortable with him, but he did not
take a stand and interfere with Tom's dreams. Bill was concerned
about changing the character of their business. He was afraid Tom
was following a darker part of himself that Bill did not understand.
Tom was acting like a boy by seeing what he could get away with, not
like a man by providing value in the family tradition.

The ambitious young man convinced Tom that Bill wasn't aggres-
sive enough and was impeding the company's growth. Bill's sleep became fitful. His wife noticed trouble between the brothers where there
had previously been great respect. Rather than providing more to
their customers or increasing the company's capacity to serve more
people, the company began to exploit them by giving less service and
charging more. This was not the family ethic that made Bill so proud.
Tom was less than honest with customers: making promises and de-
livering little. When the brothers argued, Bill pointed out that the
company's behavior was what people needed to be protected from.

This reminded Bill of his grandfather's warning: know where to take a stand to preserve your reputation for integrity.

Bill observed his brother being poisoned by greed and ambition. He asked Tom to reconsider his strategy. He predicted the inevitable results—that they would lose their respected reputation and their business. Tom glibly dismissed him as naive and parochial. Bill decided to leave the company. His heavy heart left him no choice. He was unwilling to compromise his standards, and he could no longer live with his brother's mood of greed. Tom could not hear what Bill was saying about integrity, standards, and family tradition.

Conflict

It was necessary to reach a financial settlement about their partnership. The brothers' family business had to be divided, and one of their friends suggested they call me. I was not surprised that by the time they called Tom and Bill were on the verge of a battle. On the basis of preliminary advice and their personal understanding of how these situations play out, they were moving into the traditional system of "confliction." It was impossible for them to move forward. Each was locked in the posture of blaming the other, insisting he was "right," his brother "wrong." Proving "I am right" became the most important part of the conflict.

The brothers were steeling for a battle. They stopped talking to each other. Each consulted his own gladiator. There was no sign of any ability to stand in the other's shoes, and no ability to be vulnerable and "real" about the situation. Their positions were polarized, and their feelings of great loss were not being recognized. They were beginning to defer to their professionals.

Meanwhile, business was at a virtual standstill. All energy was devoted to "winning" the battle. The struggle was about how much the business was worth and who would pay whom, when, and on what terms. No one was thinking about reaching a fair resolution, taking care of customers, or the future of the business. The pie they and their ancestors had so painstakingly baked was crumbling.

Both brothers were living the old paradigm: they were framing their situation as a great problem with many issues, not as a business event that required creativity to accommodate everyone in the situation.

The Attitude of Resolution

I focused on helping Bill and Tom see how continuing the battle would cost them time, money, emotional upset, a huge chunk of opportunity cost, and scars they would carry for the rest of their life. Neither of them would be devoting time to the future; there would be no time free from the emotional baggage of the past. I sensed from my initial separate conversations with each of them that preservation of brotherhood was a concern neither of them wanted to address or acknowledge. After I spoke to them, they understood that they would both be better off with a new agreement that was reached quickly. Neither could afford the financial, emotional, or spiritual cost of escalating acrimony. The message I sent them was their "wake-up call":

> "If you go to court and continue to do battle, you will end up with a new agreement. The terms will be dictated by a judge who knows very little about your situation. The decision is likely to be far less workable for each of you than one that could be designed by both of you. Please consider what I am saying very carefully. Remember the wisdom of Solomon when he quickly resolved a custody dispute by suggesting that the child be cut in two. If we work together we can design the resolution that creates value for both of you. Otherwise, by the time the war ends the business will have little value, and you will lose each other."

After discussing their expected resistance, the brothers were willing to meet with me. They had become so upset, they had nothing to lose. Getting people together is more than half the battle. Coming to the table holds the unspoken declaration "I want to resolve this matter."

When we met, tempers were hot. I thought it best to resolve the situation as quickly as possible. They agreed to continue one session until everything was addressed.

Telling The Story

The first part of the day gave each brother the opportunity to tell his story. I reminded them that it might be important to preserve their brotherhood and that the cost of not reaching an agreement together would be enormous. Each listened carefully as the other spoke without interruption. For both, it was like having their day in court. They spoke what was in their hearts. This enflamed their anger, but it also provided catharsis. It gave me a sense of where the situation was at that moment and where it might be headed. I listened to what was being said, and I also listened to what was present and *not* being said.

Completion

After the brothers had told their stories, I asked them a structured set of questions—a "completion" process that guided them across tender and volatile ground. Each spoke of being so frustrated and irritated by the other brother that it was impossible to be around him. Many harsh, almost unmentionable things were said. I facilitated the dialogue into areas of vulnerability that we all have about someone as familiar as a brother. Disappointment, shame and sorrow, and the loss of the family tradition were among these. The process was difficult, but it was also a great release. The open hostility started to diminish. They realized their camaraderie had been displaced by greed. Tears were shed, and some understanding began to surface.

When they saw what they had lost—unrealized expectations of a vision for the future—they could grieve. After their grief, they could let go and start to form a new vision for their future without the other, what I call an *agreement in principle.*

New Agreement

After the better part of a day, the brothers put their new vision of the future into an agreement. It contained what they wanted and what they would need from each other in their new business relationship.

Most important and crucial to their respective prosperity, they were both heading off on their own, using their resources to build a new future. They were no longer stuck in the past, fighting and wasting energy about what had already crumbled.

We did not just get the matter settled. We resolved the emotional issues and structured what their future relationship would be. Bill would move to another part of the state and start his own business. It was their intention to help each other have a successful business reflecting their particular values. Reaching a buy-out figure was not difficult once the emotions were addressed. They agreed not to compete with each other. Their measure of satisfaction was success in business and continuing brotherhood. Their fear was dishonoring their new agreement.

Resolution

A new form of partnership was born. These "enemies" realized their brotherhood. They became colleagues, creditors, fellow travelers who had wisdom and experience to share. Most of all, they remained brothers. The details of the business agreement were not as important as having them quickly move into the future with minimal disruption and expense. They felt good to be resolved, back in action and productivity. The heartbreak could start healing.

I assumed the responsibility of keeping everyone accountable for satisfactory resolution. It's a matter of having the patience and determination to stay on track until the resolution appears. No matter how bleak the situation looks, you must keep swimming upstream, both guiding and allowing everyone to educate each other about what the optimum outcome might be. You must hold fast that resolution will happen. That can look like position and power, but it is really about faith.

Summary

This chapter contains an example of the model in action. The story demonstrates the value of the new paradigm—seeing the bigger picture and recognizing what is being wasted in a situation. It provides some insight into the texture of resolution, as well as an example of what's possible. It tells you the value of a new perspective you can adopt. While my role in the situation was that of a paid facilitator, the same process could have been used by a friend or confidant. As the book will show, the model has wide application—both as to the situation, and who uses it.

Reflections

Think of a long-term relationship in which a situation of conflict was resolved by either your winning or your taking advantage of another. How did you feel after the thrill of victory wore thin? Did the situation come back to have consequences or repercussions you did not see when you won? Would resolution have been more enduring? Why?

Chapter Four

A Road Map for Resolving Conflict: The Resolution Model

If you want to succeed, strike out on new paths rather than travel the worn paths of accepted success.

—*John D. Rockefeller*

We don't think about the web of agreements making up our lives until we think that a collaborator has violated an explicit or implicit agreement that we believed we had. Then our internal chatter begins.

You would think that the skill of crafting clear agreements, because it is so basic to successful living, would be an element of our core curriculum, installed during our early educational process as part of our basic operating system. Unfortunately, we usually learn through suffering, when we realize we do not know what goes into an effective agreement.

The Abilene Paradox

At the outset of a transaction or relationship, it is important to be clear and detailed about where you are heading. Recently I asked

Mark, a senior manager at Visa, to share his greatest challenge. He told me that he often observed people moving into action before they knew where they were going. He wanted people to be clear about their destination before they moved into action, otherwise they end up in places where they do not want to be. In terms of the model of resolution, this concept is important for two reasons: (1) clarity on the front end of a new relationship minimizes conflict; and (2) the resolution of conflict is a new, clear agreement.

Mark's concerns are best illustrated in the classic story of the "Abilene Paradox."[5] Here's a brief version.

Six people were sitting on a porch one hot August night about 100 miles from Abilene, Texas. The temperature was 99°, and so was the humidity. Suddenly they piled into a sedan without air-conditioning, heading for Abilene. They were driving over unpaved roads, to buy ice-cream, to cool them off. As they traveled through the soupy weather, road-dust wafted into the vehicle, coating their skin. They became increasingly uncomfortable. Each wondered "whose dumb idea was it to go to Abilene."

The trip back provided little relief. They became more agitated as they returned home. The internal din of "Whose dumb idea was it?" increased to a roar as the ice-cream melted, adding stickiness to the coat of dust. When they arrived home they piled out of the vehicle as quickly as they had piled in. Immediately they started finger pointing. As they quieted down, they all realized that no one had wanted to go. They each had gone along for the ride, thinking it was a dumb idea but not wanting to say so.

How many trips to Abilene have you taken? Creating an effective agreement at the beginning of a relationship will save you many uncomfortable miles.

A Universal Model for Working With Others

Dialogue at the beginning of a relationship prevents conflict and puts all people involved on the same page. The conversation builds partnership; everyone begins with the same vision in mind. The dialogue shines light on the transaction by articulating all the details. It maximizes the chance for everyone to obtain what they want.

Although there is a fine body of work on conflict theory suggesting principles that will get you to resolution, there is no easy-to-follow model that specifies what needs to be discussed and resolved to reach an effective agreement. From my experience as a lawyer and in my work for business organizations, I developed such a model for anyone who wants to maximize his or her ability to have successful collaborations.

The model takes you through steps of a dialogue that lead to an effective agreement. It moves you through the inevitable conflicts, back to a state of resolution and productivity. Although the model is presented in a linear fashion, when you begin working with it, you will understand its artfulness and the "soft" edges of the steps in the process.

On the next page is a list of the steps followed by a short overview of each one, corresponding to the graphic representation of the steps shown below. Chapters 15 through 21 contain the detailed "how-to" for each step, along with illustrative stories and a more thorough explanation.

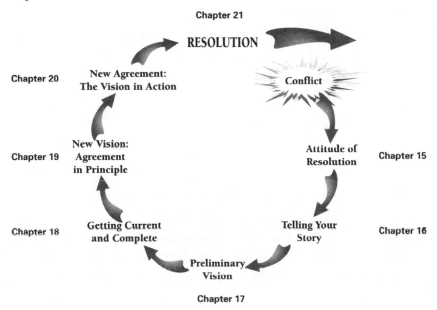

The seven steps of the resolution model are as follows:

Step 1. Developing the Attitude of Resolution

Step 2. Telling Your Story

Step 3. Listening for a Preliminary Vision of Resolution

Step 4. Getting Current and Complete

Step 5. Seeing a Vision for the Future: Agreement in Principle

Step 6. Crafting the New Agreement: Making the Vision into Reality

Step 7. Resolution: When Your Agreement Becomes Reality

As each of the steps are discussed below, remember the process that the two brothers went through in Chapter 3.

Step 1. Developing the Attitude of Resolution

The ten principles discussed in Part III hold the values that make up the attitude of resolution. This attitude is the place of beginning, a critical first step. It is not enough to mechanically go through the motions of the process without first cultivating the attitude or mood of resolution. This will not happen at once. It will take time to change the way you think. The beliefs and patterns you have about conflict took a long time to develop. They are deeply imbedded and operate in unconscious ways. It may require intention to adopt new ways of thinking about collaborators and conflict. Faith and trust in yourself and others is called for. You can accomplish it. This is the foundational step. The goal is internalizing the principles.

Step 2. Telling Your Story

The second step is telling your story and listening to all stories, including yours. It is about understanding and being understood, one of the Seven Habits of Highly Effective People that Dr. Steven Covey inspires us to cultivate.[6] There is great value in listening to the stories of others who are part of the situation. Looking for "the truth" in their story is not as important as honoring their authenticity and understanding "their truth." Developing sharp listening skills enables you to understand another's view of reality. If you learn to listen with a careful ear and honor everyone's story about a situation, you take a big step toward getting to resolution.

Step 3. Listening for a Preliminary Vision of Resolution

The third step is to start thinking about a resolution that honors all concerns in the situation. It is about shifting from the desire to win and get your way to a vision that everyone can buy into. It comes from a sense of fairness. This initial vision may change as you gather more information and learn more. You must stay with the perspective that it is as important for "them" to get what they want as it is for you to get what you want. This is the thesis in Roger Dawson's work on "power negotiating"—the most powerful way to get what you want is to make sure that others get what they want.[7] The roots of the resolution come from believing in abundance—that there is enough for everyone.

Step 4. Getting Current and Complete

The fourth step demands saying difficult, sometimes gut-wrenching things. It is about articulating what usually goes unexpressed and escaping from the emotional and intellectual prisons that keep us locked in the past. It is a way to face the good and bad in any situation and to experience and grieve for the disappointment of unrealized expectations. It is a way to put all of the detail out on the table—and choose those remnants that can be used to weave a new tapestry of resolution.

Step 5. Seeing a Vision for the Future: Agreement in Principle

Now that you have a preliminary vision, along with the information and emotional freedom provided by the completion process, you are ready for the fifth step—reaching an agreement in principle. Having looked at what other people need and noticing the cracks in your righteous position, you are ready to reach a general understanding of the resolution. This is the foundation of a new agreement. You let go of the desire for what you know will not work, and you focus on what will.

Step 6. Crafting the New Agreement: Making the Vision into Reality

In the sixth step you put specifics onto the agreement in principle. You design and construct a detailed vision of the future. The key point: you have a map, a formula for the dialogue that will maximize the potential for everyone to obtain their desired results. The more time you spend in detailing the desired results, the greater the chance to realize them.

Step 7. Resolution: When Your Agreement Becomes Reality

The seventh and final step is moving back into action. With a new agreement and a quiet, clear mind about the past, you can freely move forward, devoting your energy and intention to currently desired outcomes. You will have a new and profound sense of freedom because you have spoken all the unspeakables. You have completed the past and constructed a clear picture of the future and of the highway that will get you there. You will be empowered by the process. You are resolved.

Summary

This chapter introduces the seven-step model of resolution, a road map that enables you to operate according to the principles of the new paradigm. Chapters 15–21 will explain each step in greater detail, after you have been introduced to the principles that are the foundation of Step 1—The Attitude of Resolution.

Reflections

Make a choice to adopt the principles and practices suggested in this book. This will enable you to achieve different results in arenas of collaboration that have been problematic for you. Select a few collaborations that are not quite what you would like them to be. Commit to try the model for 21 days, the time it takes to establish a new habit. Choose the date you will begin. Notice what happens!

Part III

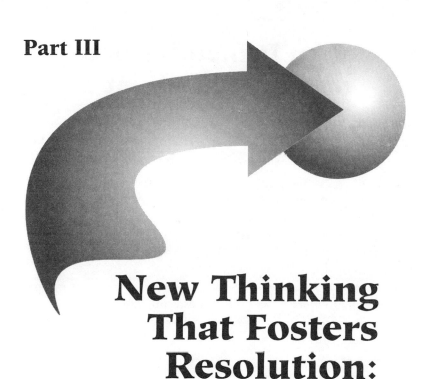

New Thinking That Fosters Resolution: Ten Principles

The steps to resolution are
of little value unless
you embrace the underlying values
driving the new practices.
Part III explains the ten principles
that make up the "new thinking"
that is the foundation of the model.

Ten Principles of a New Paradigm

OLD PARADIGM	NEW PARADIGM	CHAPTER
1. *Scarcity*	1. *Abundance*	5
2. *Wasting of Resources*	2. *Efficiency*	6
3. *Problems, Issues, Emotions*	3. *Creativity*	7
4. *Fostering Conflict*	4. *Fostering Resolution*	8
5. *Righteous Bravado, Posturing*	5. *Vulnerability*	9
6. *Short-term Adversary*	6. *Forming Long-Term Collaborations*	10
7. *Logic*	7. *Feelings and Intuition*	11
8. *Secrecy*	8. *Fully Disclosing Information and Feelings*	12
9. *Winning*	9. *Learning Through the Resolution Process*	13
10. *Defer to Professionals*	10. *Becoming ResponseAble*	14

Chapter Five

Believing in Abundance

OLD PARADIGM	NEW PARADIGM
Scarcity	*Abundance*

> *When you look at the world in a narrow way, how narrow it seems! . . . But when you look at it in a broad, generous, friendly spirit, what wonderful people you find in it.*
>
> —Horace Rutledge

The first principle—abundance—is included in and foundational for all others. If you don't believe there is "enough"—enough for you to get what you want and for others to get what they want—resolution will be very difficult. If you believe there is enough, then following the other nine principles and the steps of the model will produce resolution. It will not always be easy, but it is that simple!

Abundance: A Product of Creativity

Abundance is present in any situation because of your creative capacity. Your creative ideas are the source from which value emerges. I recently called a client who had not paid his bill. He said he did not have the funds. Instead of becoming angry, I asked about other services or property he might provide to compensate me for the value of my services. After speaking for a while, we realized he had some computer equipment worth twice the value of what I was owed that I needed and that he was not using. I was very pleased with the resolution, and so was he. This potential exists in every conflict. It's a matter of engaging in a productive dialogue so that what is needed to resolve the situation can be discovered or invented out of the creative potential that surrounds us all the time.

If the two brothers in Chapter 3 had remained narrowly focused on dividing the business, they never would have arrived at the place where their creative talent could benefit them. When they realized things were not working, they had a choice. They could fight about what they thought they had, or they could turn to each other and realize that through their prior joint and individual creative efforts they had reached the top of a mountain. From this vantage point each saw a new summit that he wanted to climb. The new summits were different, but there was no reason not to help each other.

There is no law that says we both can't get to the top of the mountain of our dreams. Why hold a position that it "must be a particular way." If you remain willing to consider a greater universe of potential solutions, you may get much more than you expect.

Abundance: The Creativity of Money

All profit, value, wealth, and accumulation result from the ideas either of one person or of a group of people combining their energy and talent. Think for a moment of a new business, a new team, or a community project that you were once a part of. The value of the business, the contribution to the larger organization, or the benefit to the community came from someplace. Microsoft started as an idea in someone's mind. The creative energy of many people coming together and the innovations they have designed have made many millionaires, and a few billionaires. The source came from an unlimited supply of abundant potential. Before Microsoft, the whole domain of PCs as personal productivity tools barely existed. It does now!

It's your choice! If you choose the principle of abundance when you come together to resolve a conflict, you can step into a field of enormous potential. It's not you *or* me; it's not us *or* them. No matter the situation, we can all have what we want if we tap into the abundant supply available to all of us. The resolution may look different than our initial expectation. So what?

Remember, the glass is half full!

Summary

The Principle of Abundance is the keystone for resolutionary thinking. There is no limit to what creativity can produce. We can apply the same principles of unlimited creativity to solving problems and resolving conflict as we do to new ventures.

Reflections

As you look at the remaining nine principles and review all of the case studies and examples, look for the perspective of abundance. Notice all the places in your life where you have been conditioned by a perspective of scarcity. Does that kind of thinking limit your potential?

Chapter Six

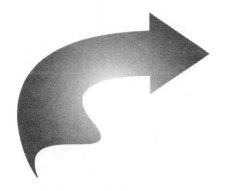

Using Resources Efficiently

OLD PARADIGM	NEW PARADIGM
Wasting Resources	*Using Resources Efficiently*

A man who dares to waste one hour has not discovered the value of life.

—Darwin

People who are working together often waste resources because they do not have a clearly articulated vision of where they are going and how they will get there. They waste more resources resolving the inevitable conflicts that surface.

That was my belief when I started practicing law 25 years ago. It hasn't changed. This is true for all types of collaborations—business partnerships, joint ventures, intracompany teams, and employee-manager and professional-client relationships. It's especially true for lovers and spouses. The waste is increasing. Look at our litigiousness.

At the beginning, when you are very excited about the new venture or relationship, the "standard" way of doing things asks you to focus on all the things that can go wrong. Once you scare yourself by thinking about all the "what ifs" ("what if this . . . " and "what if that . . . "), your lawyer may do his or her best to "protect" you from any

nasty things your new partner might do to you. This has the predictable effect of creating an adversary relationship before you even
begin working together. This can shift hopeful, positive expectations
to distrust and polarization. It can get people so turned off that a well-
intentioned collaboration never happens. You don't even have a "honeymoon" with your new collaborator, let alone time to enjoy it. It's
not my intention to blame lawyers; they're doing the best job they
have been trained to do.

The inefficiency gets worse. If you end up in a disagreement that
you can't easily resolve, you may end up looking for truth and justice
in a courtroom. That will cost you in many ways. You find yourself
not communicating with a partner or spouse, not taking care of the
real business of your life, and wasting more resources. In Chapter 2
we noted that the waste of resources includes direct cost, opportunity
cost, continuity cost, and emotional cost.

The two brothers in Chapter 3 were on the road to wasting resources. If they had not taken the course of the new paradigm, they
would have followed the advice of their well-meaning lawyers who were
doing the best they knew how. The brothers may have wasted a few years
trying to gain a strategic advantage within a context of traditional litigation. They would have suffered the waste of losing what they expected
their business to produce and the diminished value of the business; the
waste of the direct cost of two sets of lawyers and forensic experts; the
waste of what they might have produced if their attention was focused
on productivity; the waste of losing the community they had built; and
the waste of the emotional resources drained by the conflict.

Let's compare this to what actually happened. Within a short period of time they came together and efficiently resolved a difficult situation. Each moved on with his own life: minimum expenses,
minimum time, minimum emotional energy.

Creating Agreements Efficiently

The adversarial mind-set pervades our thinking in many collaborative
situations. We overlook the value of doing our best to make sure the

"partnership" will be effective. The process of putting an effective agreement in place requires addressing many specific aspects of what you will do together, including acknowledging that conflict will occur and mapping out a strategy for dealing with it. The conflict prevention happens when you agree on how you will agree and disagree, inevitable aspects of a working relationship.

If you efficiently detail your agreement at the beginning of a relationship or when inevitable conflict occurs, it has extraordinary value. Inefficiency often comes from not knowing what goes into a good agreement. Having a template for an agreement creates efficiency. You do not have to reinvent the wheel each time. You know the elements that have to be discussed, and you talk about them. If everyone can get on the same page at the beginning, time is not wasted with fits and starts about who will do what. A full and complete conversation at the beginning enables you to efficiently decide if it is appropriate to move forward. This prevents wasting resources on a doomed transaction.

When I first developed the agreement template that is discussed in Chapter 20, I felt like a kid with a new toy. I was thrilled by the surprised reaction people had when I would ask a few questions of each person in a collaboration and the next day produce an agreement that satisfied everyone. It expressed the participants' vision of what they wanted to happen, not how they would be protected if things go wrong.

Creating an Efficient Collaboration

Getting a successful project up and running is an exercise in forming a collaborative team. That requires going through some conflict, but not as much as traditional wisdom would have you believe. Teams go through four stages: forming, storming, norming, and performing. The conflict involved in passing through these stages cannot be avoided, but it can be minimized if (1) a team agreement is put in place at the beginning, and (2) everyone is willing to use the principles and model in this book and quickly engage in conversations for resolution when conflict arises.

I used to withdraw quickly from projects that were diverting time and energy from a declared mission. I noticed that members of the team were more concerned with personal power and individual success than with accomplishing stated objectives. I have learned that if you can stay focused on agreed-upon goals and objectives while operating from shared vision and values, all else will fall into place. The challenge: .learning to let go of ego concerns. A key is to embrace a mind-set of abundance—everyone can win without the need for a loser. Keeping our eyes on the big picture, seeing the forest through the trees, and losing certain battles for the sake of the larger cause are clichés, but they emphasize that continuing is usually more efficient than leaving, despite the temporary conflict. Starting over is usually very inefficient.

If efficient front-end agreements and resolution processes are created at the beginning of a project, they will keep a team focused on goals. Although you never know what will happen on a journey, it is better not to begin unless you can maximize your chances for success.

Summary

Present standard practice wastes enormous amounts of resources in both reaching agreement and resolving conflict. A key principle of the new paradigm is to conserve human and material resources by making the agreement and resolution process efficient.

Reflections

Think of a situation in which you believed you were wasting time or material resources. What was the reason for the waste? How could you have done it more efficiently? Do you think a clearly expressed vision and an explicit agreement would have helped?

Chapter Seven

Being Creative

OLD PARADIGM	NEW PARADIGM
Problem, Issue, Emotion	*Being Creative*

Imagination is more important than knowledge.

—*Albert Einstein*

Most people are emotionally upset when confronted with conflict and differences. They have adopted the prevailing attitude that all things should be perfect, smooth, and without rough edges. Shouldn't they? Aren't we entitled to be upset when they aren't?

Conflict as an Ordinary and Expected Phenomenon

When I listen to businesspeople and lawyers talk, I usually hear them speaking about the problems and issues that upset, concern, or worry them.

Many people have difficulty accepting that life is filled with surprises, conflict, disappointment, and unmet expectations. These things happen—consistently and predictably. This phenomenon was elegantly expressed by an infant I recently saw at the airport. Mom was preparing the child for a feeding, and she pulled out a beautiful embroidered bib. Inscribed in large bold letters were the words

"SPIT HAPPENS."

Yes, SPIT happens! What you do with it, how you deal with it, your attitude toward it—that marks the quality of your life.

Have you ever been in a recurrent conflict with a family member or colleague? Each time the conflict jumps out at you, it is impossible to think about a creative solution. You are gripped by your own emotion, and from within this strong "reaction," there is little possibility of creativity.

For example, one of my college roommates never cleaned his room. I could not think about creative resolutions because when I saw the clutter, I immediately had a strong emotional reaction. A few years later I was confronted with a similar situation. By then, I had trained myself to say "STOP" as I observed myself moving into a strong emotional reaction. Stopping enables me to focus on a creative solution before the trigger is pulled and the emotion explodes, rendering me useless.

There is no return on investing unnecessary emotional energy. We do not have unlimited capacity. As my partner Irving used to say, "Stewart, you cannot unpunch someone." Learning to treat conflict as ordinary and expected is the goal. When you learn that, you can focus your resources on creative solutions.

Creativity in Action

Observing how we talk to ourselves is a key part of learning to live in the principle of creativity. Programming yourself not to use the word *problem* when confronted by any situation that has potential for conflict is a useful tack. The trick is framing the situation as an opportunity to demonstrate your creativity. Before your emotions render you useless, think about what would be the most effective action. When someone tells you he or she has a problem to deal with just smile and say, "No, we have an opportunity to demonstrate how creative we can be." The key is how we talk to ourselves. If we want to see the glass as half full, then our internal conversation must say that—we must say to ourselves that the situation is an opportunity, and not a problem.

Let's look at three examples of creativity in action.

Broaden Your Perspective

Both of the brothers in Chapter 3 were following the traditional route. The lawyers they consulted saw this as a series of legal issues to be resolved: Who had more voting stock in the corporation? Who was violating his obligations to the organization? Was anyone abandoning his responsibilities? Was anyone wasting the assets of the organization? Is there any entitlement to a payout? What is the value of the business? Dealing with those mixed legal and business valuation issues is enough to keep a small army of lawyers and forensic accountants busy for a while. No one was looking at the situation from the practical perspective of creatively dealing with a going concern in a way that would preserve value.

I had no bias or orientation about what was supposed to happen. There was no restriction limiting my thinking about a potential outcome. The major focus was coming up with a resolution that honored the concerns expressed by the brothers.

Even though there might be fighting, you don't have to see it as a fight; even though there is willfulness, you don't have to see the situation as a test of wills; even though there are legal issues, you don't have to see the situation as a legal battle; even though there were accounting issues, you don't have to see it as an accounting problem.

In the new paradigm, the conflict is seen as an exercise in creative problem solving. That led the two brothers beyond the value judgments that create issues, problems, and emotions. It coaxed them to the terrain of creativity. They came up with the solution because they followed the new paradigm of collaboration. We arrived at a landscape no expert they consulted had explored because it was not within the discipline of their profession.

Avoid the Either/or Mind-set

Liza and Kathy were partners in a successful consulting and training business. After ten years together they reached a crossroad. The question they faced was whether to hire additional consultants or retain their current size and select higher quality projects.

Liza was clear that the best course was selecting bigger clients. She did not want all the headaches of having employees. Kathy was certain about hiring a few more consultants to leverage their existing business. These two intelligent, competent individuals were both sure of their own direction. Each was correct about the right path—for her. But that was not the question. The question was what they should do for the business and for their partnership.

As time passed, Liza and Kathy became resentful of the other's position. Even though they loved their work and their clients, each was experiencing the chatter of wasting brain space with thoughts of how to manipulate the situation to her advantage. The crisis came to a head when Kathy found out Liza turned down a request to train a multidivision computer manufacturer in their proprietary communication model; it was not a high-quality prospect in Liza's opinion. Kathy was crazed by Liza's decision; Liza was unfazed by Kathy's outrage. Liza believed she had made the right decision. She had, for Liza.

After three days of lost productivity and not speaking to Liza, Kathy called me. I asked her what she wanted. Kathy's response was typical. She just wanted to put this behind them and get back to work. Liza had the same response when I spoke to her. For both of them the pain was so great that having a particular resolution was not as important as resolution itself. I let them think about that over the weekend and scheduled a meeting for Monday morning.

On Monday I asked if they could live with the fact that they were both right. They said yes, if they could get back to work! I asked them to design the structure of the business they wanted to operate. I asked them to exchange plans and let me know how they would participate in the other's plan. Then they decided on their roles. I then asked if there was a reason they couldn't live with the jobs they had selected in the other's design. They were OK with their roles. Good, I said. You have worked this out.

What was their plan? Kathy managed the expanded number of consultants, and Liza focused on more senior projects. They both returned to the joy, productivity, and fulfillment that made the partnership great. They did not compromise. Each had her concerns taken care of. This is a good example of how often we step into an "either/or mind-set"—either you get yours, or I get mine. It is important to remember that if you refuse to see the other person as the enemy and you each engage your creativity, often everyone can have what he or she wants. Seeing the world as abundant—the first principle—helps a lot.

An Organic Agreement

Selena and Sergio came from traditional backgrounds. It was agreed that Selena would teach school and put Sergio through graduate school. To an observer it looked like a very conservative union. Aside from their marriage vows, they had only one explicit agreement: they agreed to stay together as long as it remained fun.

Their marriage thrived for ten years. They were fulfilled, prosperous and had a wonderful home and many friends. After ten years each caught a dose of wanderlust. There was more angst and confinement than the fun they had agreed to. They decided to separate. They allowed their relationship, and the agreement that contained it, to grow—no lawyers, no high drama, no bitterness. They remain the best of friends, being there for each other as the need arose.

They have allowed their friendship to develop creatively, based on their personal needs. Rather than evaluate and judge each other, they have chosen to honor the profound respect each has for the other's personal process. Neither one knows where the connection will lead. The only certainty is that they stay in touch as they ride the waves of change and transition in their respective lives. Rather than evaluating what goes on between them against an external standard of what is "supposed" to be, they allow themselves the freedom to create in uncharted waters. Trusting yourself enough to paint on a blank canvas is the essence of creativity.

Summary

On the basis of their domain of expertise, most professionals and businesspeople are conditioned to think in terms of issues and problems. The experts try to fix problems in a way that satisfies their professional standards of what is right. Most people have a belief system that says conflict and disagreement are bad. When you combine the restrictive approach of these two phenomena with the fear of consequences of conflict, the chance of getting stuck multiplies. Moving to a broader field of creativity enhances the potential for satisfactory resolution because it removes the constraints and broadens the field of potential solutions.

Reflections

Think of a few situations in your life that were not resolved to your satisfaction. Reflect on the way you approached them. If you were not limited by beliefs about what you thought proper, right, or wrong, how might you have resolved the situations differently? Now think of some current conflicts. What potential creative resolutions do you see when you remove the limitations of your own thinking? Start implementing your ideas today!

Chapter Eight

PRINCIPLE 4

Fostering Resolution

OLD PARADIGM	NEW PARADIGM
Fostering Conflict	*Fostering Resolution*

If you do not wish to be prone to anger, do not feed the habit; give it nothing which may tend to its increase. At first, keep quiet and count the days when you were not angry: "I used to be angry every day, then every other day: next, every two, then every three days!" and if you succeed in passing thirty days, sacrifice to the gods in thanksgiving.

—Epictetus

Traditional systems of conflict resolution are often like spraying gasoline on a fire. The flames get hotter and higher. Although there are situations in which the teeth of our legal system are essential (see Chapter 24), many standard interventions like suits, countersuits, motions, depositions, and interrogatories are "courtly" games few can afford to play. The following things often happen when you get involved with standard methods for resolving conflict.

1. Your lawyer does the "lawyering"—filing lawsuits and the like.

2. Your conflict is classified to fit within a legal theory, deflecting the inquiry from the underlying personal conflict.

3. Your lawyer will likely instruct you to stop talking to the other people involved.

4. The goal becomes winning, not resolution or preserving the relationship.

5. Little is done to address your emotional pain and your grief over the lost expectation you anticipated in the transaction or relationship.

6. The practice of hourly billing is a conflict of interest that does not motivate resolution.

7. Your conflict becomes your lawyer's case. Ego and greed may take it places other than resolution.

8. The process wears you down. The technical rules of the "legal game" may keep out the most important facts and preclude the most important inquiry.

9. It may take years to get before a judge. When you finally get there, the judge wants you to settle. Judges prefer matters that focus on novel issues or impact many people. Or you may get a judge who is not very smart.

10. Finding truth is often elusive. Justice can be a roll of the dice, not found in a courtroom.

11. Getting the case "settled" is more important than the quality of the resolution—resolving the real concerns.

All of these aspects of the current system for resolving conflict can make the conflict worse.

Fostering Resolution With Collaboration

In the new paradigm, reaching agreements and addressing differences take place within a context of resolution. Creative, collaborative systems for making agreements and resolving conflicts are the norm. Reaching agreement is no longer an adversarial negotiation. Negotiating is about creating a composite, shared vision of the desired outcome. Built into the agreement is the understanding that disagreement will happen. Dealing with disagreements is framed as an opportunity to deepen the agreement, not a feared breakdown. All are inside the same circle, standing together, shoulder to shoulder, wondering how best to take care of their shared concerns while envisioning together the future they want to create.

The two brothers followed the paradigm of fostering resolution. It was opposite from the path their lawyers selected. They were both told to stop communicating—that the path to resolution was a court battle. This made it much worse than it had to be.

Instead, the brothers used a process designed to diffuse conflict and move quickly to resolution. Each told his story and then listened to the other's story, so each brother would know what was happening in the other's mind. This provided venting and catharsis. Next, they went through a "completion" process: all that needed to be said to get to the core of the conflict was voiced. That facilitated their grieving the loss of their expectations for the family business. Then they could move forward. Getting every aspect of the conflict in the open is essential. But if they had not talked to each other, nothing would be left of their business. That does not foster resolution.

Many lawyers make a great living within the systems for resolving conflict. Sometimes they provide an invaluable service. But in most situations there is a better way. Whenever a new judge is appointed, I say to myself, "Four mediators would foster much more resolution." Fortunately, mine is not the only voice speaking for reform.

Summary

Current standard practice often makes things worse by fanning the fires of conflict. Under the new paradigm it is important to take steps that dissipate the conflict and move to resolution without making things worse.

Reflections

If you have ever been involved in litigation, spend ten minutes writing about what the process was like and your emotions as you were in it. If you have not been involved in litigation, find someone who has and speak to them about what the process was like for them. Specifically ask how it affected the conflict in terms of intensity, duration, levels of trust, ability to work together, and emotional release. Ask if the person was satisfied with the result and whether the situation was resolved.

Chapter Nine

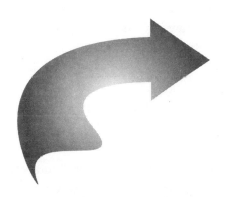

PRINCIPLE 5

Becoming Vulnerable

OLD PARADIGM   **NEW PARADIGM**
Righteous Bravado and Posturing   *Vulnerability*

Show Up
Pay Attention
Tell Your Truth
Don't Be Attached to the Outcome

—The Four Fold Way, *Angelis Arrien, Ph.D.*[8]

Under the accepted paradigm, people in conflict posture. They play games. They horse around. The focus is more about being right than being effective. Winning has become the highest value. No one gets points for candor!

Many of our role models come from television. *Dallas, L.A. Law, Perry Mason,* and the O.J. Simpson trial are examples. The bravado we see, and often follow, seems cool as a sound bite, but it doesn't get us the results we want. Saying "I'll see you in court" may feel great in the moment because we see the hero do it on TV, but it can be like going down the rabbit hole with Alice. We may do something in the moment to save face, be cool, or act macho in an uncomfortable situation. We want to make sure we "look good." Often we end up in a more difficult place because of what we have done in the name of bravado.

Reprogramming Yourself to Be Vulnerable

People often act from bravado because they have never seen another way. Soft-spoken vulnerability, and the honesty and self disclosure attached to it, do not sell movies, books, or TV shows. There are few visible role models for this behavior. And yet, in my workshops around the country, the qualities that audiences consistently mention as admirable are honesty, listening, authenticity, lack of ego, and understanding another perspective.

Because of the cultural pressures to be otherwise, being vulnerable is not very acceptable. But vulnerability is an easy, natural way to be. Being vulnerable is not being weak. Being vulnerable is being your real, authentic self. Getting beyond your initial resistance is challenging. But once beyond that resistance, it is the easiest behavior to adopt.

What I mean by *vulnerability* is summed up at the beginning of this chapter by Dr. Arrien as the four guides for all human interaction. You are fully present, without an act, story, or angle. You tell your truth without the need to have the outcome be a certain way. That is a great way to stay centered and empty of the kind of emotional attachment that will get you in trouble. There is no acting or scheming; you are simply yourself. It's easy because you don't worry about being consistent with your previous "act" or story; you don't have to second-guess yourself or posture. You just show up and tell your truth.

The two brothers did not initially come to the table in an open place of vulnerability. The resolution process they chose took them to a place of vulnerability they did not expect to go. To achieve resolution it was essential to tap into areas of vulnerability surrounding their relationship as brothers. It is a commonly understood psychological phenomenon that before you can move through an emotional trauma, you must grieve the loss. But the grieving can't happen unless you go to a place of vulnerability. Proceeding traditionally never gets you to vulnerability because it requires bravado and posturing. The brothers started on that path because they thought it was their only option. They found a better way.

Opening to Vulnerability

Maria and Scott were convinced that after years of searching they had found the mates who would fulfill their dreams. They constructed an explicit agreement for all areas of their life. This document, in great detail, put into words their vision for their future.

The unique feature of the agreement was the absence of an "out" clause. Because each had suffered the pain of failed relationships, they wanted to minimize that risk. But in the midst of the passion, promise, and expectation, they had created a contract marriage. These two free spirits designed a prison for themselves. Because of their integrity and the strength of their commitment, they tried to live within their agreement. But despite best intentions they were having a very difficult time, made more so by their also being business partners.

They opened to the deepest levels of vulnerability as they worked with therapists, counselors, consultants and other well-meaning professionals to find a way to make their relationship functional. After five years they decided to renegotiate their agreement, despite their "written in stone" promises. They agreed to separate their professional and personal lives. Letting go was as painful as the joy of coming together had been. They learned the wisdom of the organic quality of any relationship. They have no unfinished business or emotional baggage. Their vulnerability left nothing unsaid.

Because of our culture's prevalent role models, it will take generations to shift our attitudes about humility and vulnerability. People are not used to being open with each other. Looking good and using sound bites are empty substitutes for sharing truth. The following process is an excellent vehicle for helping people open to their vulnerability.

The Truth Circle

The Truth Circle is a process that generates honest communication, a key ingredient of vulnerability. It is very effective in building work teams and with families. It uses a "Talking Stick," an artifact that confers on the holder the right to talk while everyone listens. A group sits in a circle and a topic is chosen for speaking the truth. The Talking Stick is passed around three times. At first people are uncomfortable, but as they warm to the process, their truth emerges. It is a great way to invite people into an experience of vulnerability. We need the practice, because given our cultural conditioning, being vulnerable is counterintuitive.

Summary

Posturing and righteous bravado do not support resolution. They keep you distant from real concerns that need addressing. But you have been programmed by cultural role models. You must learn, through practice, the power and simplicity of authentic vulnerability.

Reflections

Think about a time when you were posturing. Did it help you resolve the situation? If you had been forthcoming, would the situation have ended differently? Would the result have been more to your liking? Is there a current situation in which you could show more vulnerability? How might things be different if you were?

Chapter Ten

PRINCIPLE 6

Forming Long-Term Collaborations

OLD PARADIGM	NEW PARADIGM
Short-term Adversary	*Long-term Collaborations*

The man who gets the most satisfactory results is not always the man with the most brilliant single mind, but rather the man who can best co-ordinate the brains and talents of his associates.

—W. Alton Jones

We are conditioned to think in terms of a short-term horizon, an immediate victory. We see only this quarter's bottom line, not this year's—let alone next year's or the next decade's.

Fear is often our driver. If fear is your prevalent emotional state, any situation can become adversarial. Fear precludes trust. When we fear, other people become adversaries whom we want to control and conquer. They are the enemy. The saddest aspect of this paradigm is that it automatically, unconsciously operates between people who want to collaborate.

The Now Culture

We come by this short-term, adversarial mind-set honestly. We have been influenced by an era of "Lone-Rangerism" — solo-riding, conquer-the-west, rugged-individual, Marlboro-man, immediate-gratification, this-quarter, "me" generation! No wonder the notion of teams, collaboration, and virtual organizations are creating havoc in many organizations. We are asking for vast changes in the way people view others while our personal programming is driving us to be top-gun, king-of-the-hill, victorious individuals—now! The patience it takes to work with others is what we really need, but it's not part of the way we have been conditioned.

Winning is deeply embedded in our national psyche. The word *win* is synonymous with success. Unfortunately, it also implies the corresponding "lose." Even though the term *win-win* is used in many places, most of us think "for me to win, you must lose." Though win-win speak is pervasive in organizations, the idea of everyone winning is not yet an operational principle people fully embrace. Though we say the words, our bodies do not believe or fully understand them. This is a great source of inner conflict, and the confusion pulls people in opposite directions.

The New Culture of Collaboration

I see the new paradigm as a vision of two people, standing shoulder to shoulder, viewing a situation of potential conflict. Under the old paradigm they would be squared off, face to face, confronting each other. In the new paradigm they are looking at the situation together, wondering how *they* will meet the challenge. They think of themselves as collaborators, co-creators jointly designing the most favorable outcome. They remain in a relationship, building and deepening trust as their collaboration develops, forged and tempered by the challenges of conflict and differences.

Both know that no matter what, from a broad perspective, they want the same outcome—a successful venture or relationship with a conflict resolution process that is respectful. They look together for the vessel that is large enough to hold and satisfy all the concerns that each of them has in the situation. They approach tasks, no matter how difficult, with a minimum of angst and emotion, and with the elegance of knowing that they will honor the challenge by caring about the long-term impact on all stakeholders, including themselves. Long-term impact is key. Whatever the situation, they do not see their relationship as a short-term, one-shot deal. They view situations with a longer horizon. Let's look at long-term collaboration within several circumstances.

The Legal Community

After practicing law with the New Jersey attorney general's office, I joined a law firm in a small New Jersey town. This was in the early 1970s, just before the population of lawyers exploded. I had to accept that the lawyer who was on the opposite side of a case today might be on my side in the future. Since the legal community was small, taking a short-term perspective would come around to bite me. This encouraged civility. A few years later I moved to Manhattan. Because the population of lawyers was so large, most lawyers had a short-term perspective. They assumed they would never deal with you again. I resisted making the adjustment because it meant that no one could be trusted.

A short-term perspective violates standards of ethics and fair play. Feeling good about yourself, which impacts your health and well-being, requires a longer view. In terms of your relationship to yourself, you're in it for the long haul. As John Kabat-Zinn says, "Wherever you go, there you are."[9] Taking the long view requires adopting the mind-set that you will be working with this person in the future. Make believe that you live in the same small town. More and more, as a result of technology, you do; it's called a *global village*. Make sure you won't feel compelled to cross the street out of embarrassment when someone is walking toward you, or when you run into him or her in the supermarket or at a PTA meeting.

Teammates

The aerospace plant where Raj and Ted were engineers was being re-organized into a team environment. They had known each other for about three years. They never exchanged more than a nod because they had a strong negative reaction to each other. Neither of them knew why, but they knew the dislike was mutual. Now they were on the same team, required to work together.

For six weeks they skirted the tension as the team organized. Then they were on the same project, asked to jointly produce designs for a key engine component. They both complained to their wives and to the team coach. Their wives just listened. The coach said that learning how to work together was part of learning how to be a good team player, especially if you don't like a teammate. That did not make them feel any better or resolve their struggle.

As they worked together and observed each other, slowly at first but with gathering momentum, respect grew. In working together they began to acknowledge each other's competence. As they became more comfortable, they found shared common interests, including a similar sense of humor. They became the backbone of their team, guiding others to greater levels of productivity and satisfaction. As engineers they observed how repulsion transformed into attraction. They said it was about going beyond their emotional reaction to a place of deeper understanding. They came to this because: (1) they had no choice about working together, (2) their coach suggested they observe and reserve their judgments and emotional reactions, and (3) they had to think of a long-term horizon.

The Marriage Contract

After a traditional courtship, Lee decided he wanted to marry Kyung. Although she loved him, Kyung was concerned about marriage. She had had a very unstable childhood. Because of her background, a condition of her marrying Lee was that they not have children. This was her bottom-line position: end of story, no discussion, issue closed. Lee agreed, and they were married.

Seven years later Lee, with more than a little apprehension about approaching his wife, decided he wanted kids. Lee asked Kyung to take another look at the decision she made seven years earlier. He was smart in the way he framed the situation. He didn't make Kyung wrong about the decision she had made. He didn't make a demand. Lee asked her to revisit the choice after acknowledging that the choice she had made seven years ago was the best choice for her at the time.

Instead of digging in her heels, calling her lawyer, or just saying "no," Kyung agreed to reconsider. This was not easy given her history, but there had been many changes in her life. Kyung and Lee had both established professional careers. As a result, Kyung had a strong inner foundation, something she did not have as a child. Even if the marriage failed, she knew she could sustain herself and her children. The circumstance she had grown up in no longer existed. The reason not to have children was no longer a concern. Rather than hold onto her "position," Kyung was willing to revisit the choice she had made.

Twenty-five years later Kyung is very pleased with her change of heart. Although the marriage ended, her children are the joy of her life. She is happy with the new choice she made. The best agreements are organic. They grow over the long term.

Friendship

Friendship is a classic example of the principle of "long-termness." All valuable relationships go through cycles. A friend once said, "I really admire long-distance runners." She was commenting on the ability to ride out the rough spots of disagreement that inevitably arise in friendships. It's part of the process when you have a long-term horizon.

It would be easier if we could transcend our emotions as we go through disagreements. But if you have experienced the joy of long-term associations, you know that in the long run the upheavals look small compared to the richness that friendship brings.

A Longer Term Perspective

Our travel and mobility as a culture contributes to our anxiety and feelings of aloneness. A sense of separateness perpetuates the case with which we blow others off. When we lived in smaller villages, we had to go through the conflict and come out the other side. There was no place to run. I think it's important to put back in place the context of having to live with people for the long term. We must live with our own response to the way we act toward others.

In the two brothers' situation, the longer term perspective of brothers for life was voiced. Although they did not fully buy into it at first, they understood it was important. As the process unfolded they came to appreciate the longer term perspective. Because there is little concern for consequences when a short-term perspective is operative, things are skewed. A sense of continuity makes most people feel good. Richness, depth, and the ability to produce long-term results come from associations that go through cycles. It is important for people to reflect on this when experiencing short-term difficulty. That perspective helps us get what we really want—sustained long-term relationships.

Summary

You can choose to operate from a short-term or a long-term perspective. If you think and act as if a collaboration will be long term, you will feel good about the relationship and yourself. You never know when the relationship will take on long-term significance, or when you will have to face the other person in your neighborhood. Remember—we all live in a global village!

Reflections

Think about a situation in which you either were taken advantage of or took advantage of someone. How did it feel? What emotions are generated by the situation? How would you act differently if you could do it over? How might you act in a similar situation in the future? Would you treat your neighbor the same way? Why not?

Chapter Eleven

Relying on Feelings and Intuition

OLD PARADIGM	NEW PARADIGM
Logical	*Feelings and Intuition*

When dealing with people, remember you are not dealing with creatures of logic, but with creatures of emotion, creatures bristling with prejudice and motivated by pride and vanity.

—Dale Carnegie

Although attitudes are changing, under the current paradigm most people still accept that the world operates on the premise of logic. Aristotle and Newton would be proud of how we follow their basic cognitive precepts of how the world works. Everything fits into a category, A flows into B, and consequences are predictable.

Beyond the Five Senses

On the basis of my observations of what is being written and what "traditional" institutions are experimenting with (alternative and eastern forms of medicine are good examples), I believe we may be on the verge of stepping onto a new foundation. The existing paradigm of "scientific method" has run to the end of its course. In this global village, we are facing many challenges whose solutions are so complex that new theoretical models are needed for the solutions and resolutions to our current challenges.

A wonderful example of this kind of inquiry is the best-seller *Leadership and the New Science* by Margaret Wheatley, a businessperson, consultant, and professor.[10] Dr. Wheatley noticed that most of the fundamental principles around which we build organizations and institutions are grounded in Newtonian Logic. This characterizes the world by "materialism and reductionism—a focus on things other than relationships." Using Newtonian logic was leading edge thinking at the time the fundamental principles were adopted.

To see what is at the leading edge of thinking today, Dr. Wheatley decided to explore current scientific developments in various disciplines. She found that in all the natural sciences, current accepted paradigms have gone way beyond Newton. The foundational assumptions on which we have built our institutions and organizations have been transcended. *Chaos* is often the operative principle. Because scientific theory has always stood firmly as the foundation for organizational theory, perhaps it's time to bring our organizations and institutions up to date with the current "scientific thinking."

Under the old paradigm and congruent with previous scientific thinking, we thought of facts and evidence in terms of the five physical senses—sight, sound, touch, smell, and taste. Today we know there is much more. In the new paradigm we can take into consideration feeling, emotion, and intuition.

This change is illustrated by the use of psychics by a number of police departments to help solve major crimes or to find missing people. Nancy Reagan's use of astrologers in the White House and Hillary Clinton's consultation with Jean Houston, a noted New Age guru, are good examples of new paradigm thinking. A professional mediation journal recently had a feature article that used the metaphor of mediator as "trickster," compared to the generally accepted notion of mediator as "professional" who always follows consistent and accepted professional standard operating theories. *Trickster* was not meant in a derogatory way, but to indicate the wider range of options.[11]

In domains previously thought to be grounded only in the world of logic, we are now allowing a broader spectrum of our "human-beingness" to be recognized as operative and important. This applies to resolving conflict in two important ways:

1. We can rely on feelings and intuition in getting to resolution.

2. We can use feelings and intuition as a factor for determining that resolution has been reached.

I remember thinking "blasphemy" when I started telling my legal clients that their written agreements were not as important as their feeling of whether they could trust another person. Even though my profession was steeped in the tradition of writings, to me trust was much more important than a tightly drafted contract. In the model of resolution in Part IV, I discuss the "phenomenon" of agreement. This is a heartfelt assessment of whether agreement exists after two or more people engage in the "process" of discussing essential elements that make up their agreement. You can say all the right words, it can look tidy, and still not constitute an agreement because something is missing at a gut level. There is no covenant.

When I work with intimate personal relationships—executives, partners, family businesses, divorces—I will not address financial and property issues until clients go through the completion processes of the conflict resolution model, a process designed to have them confront the difficult emotional aspects of the breakdowns in their working relationships. I know that the emotional pain is the real cause of the difficulty. Until you grieve, you cannot get beyond the conflict. When starting out on a new venture, one of the most important disclosures is "fears or concerns" about the transaction. Surfacing those emotions and addressing them are keys to crafting a covenantal agreement, one that will last.

In the two brothers' situation, emotions were highly charged. Unless emotional release was provided, no chance at an effective resolution was possible. All that would continue to happen, as it so often does, are people acting out their unconscious reactions and unexpressed emotions. We must learn to acknowledge the presence of these strong emotions and provide the place for them to surface. Absent venting, resolution will never happen.

Trusting Partners

Carol and Steven were joyous about the prospect of working together. They had "grown up" as professional trainers for the same Silicon Valley high-tech company. They admired and respected each other. Each had run their own business for about four years. Both were tired of working alone. When they ran into each other at an association meeting, they had a long conversation.

They talked about the challenges of working alone and the responsibility of carrying the entire show on one set of shoulders. They were doing the same things—custom-designed training for new subscribers of specialized management software. If they joined forces, the economies of scale would be substantial.

Quickly, and with a great deal of exuberance, they decided to be partners. The partnership agreement consisted of a handshake and an agreement to work out all the details as they came up. Through ups and downs, arguments and admiration, they have learned to work things out by listening and accepting different approaches. The partnership has thrived for five years, without any formal explicit agreement. Carol and Steve attribute their success to the respect, trust, and thankfulness they have for their work and to the pleasure and joy of the collaboration.

They relish the joy of painting on a blank canvas each time they make decisions. It was suggested they craft a formal partnership agreement. To date they have declined. They resisted because things are working so well. The artist in me understands. When something is working well and feels right, leave it alone—just enjoy it!

I think that we are all emotional creatures. I no longer believe people who say they can be objective. We are all subjective. The challenge is knowing what our bias is so we can factor it into the equation.

Summary

When dealing with people, you must factor in emotions because they are present in all situations. In more and more arenas, the nonlinear, nonrational is accepted.

Reflections

Examine the areas of your life that are not run by pure logic and rational analysis. Are these perceptual systems valuable for you? Are they important? In what ways?

Chapter Twelve

Disclosing Information and Feelings

OLD PARADIGM	NEW PARADIGM
Hoarding and Controlling Information	*Full Disclosure*

If there is nothing worthwhile to hide, then secrecy will earn the appropriate mistrust without providing any benefits.

—Edward DeBono[12]

Under the current paradigm, information is king. Whoever has it can hoard, use, and manipulate it. Nondisclosure—providing limited access and cutting off communication—is an accepted way of conducting business. But this game of nondisclosure dilutes the ability to get to resolution.

The Raw Material for Resolution

When disagreement erupts, the flow of information halts. People stop talking. Documents are not shared until required. This is unfortunate. Conflict and disagreement are the clearest signs that more, not less, information needs to be exchanged. Information and discussion, facts and ideas shared, are the raw material from which resolution emerges.

Cutting the flow ensures conflict, delay, and lack of consensus about the outcome.

A rich parallel comes from the business community. Traditionally, "management" has held onto information—strategic, competitive, and especially, financial. A few years ago a company called Springfield Remanufacturing ran into severe trouble. The board decided to be candid with all of the company's employees. The board members told everyone their plight: if the company did not turn around, it was on a trajectory toward financial failure. The employees responded with resourcefulness. Their innovations not only kept the company from bankruptcy, they turned the organization into a thriving, highly profitable business. The key was management providing the information employees needed to solve existing problems. They now call it "open-book" management.[13]

If you are joint venturers working on a new project with each having proprietary information, you may be hesitant to share information. But that will impede reaching the bigger joint goal. For example, if you are different drug manufacturers working on a solution to AIDS, hesitating to share what you already know will compromise the bigger goal: finding a cure. Under the new paradigm, you would readily share all the information you have. You may have to reach agreement first about allocating profit or prizes, but you understand that disclosure is essential for reaching your objective.

Clearing the Highway

A colleague recently told me about the situation that inspired him to devote all of his time to resolving conflict. Without the openness of full disclosure, this situation would never have been resolved. My colleague was asked to make a last attempt to resolve a stalled highway project. It was part of the interstate highway system started in the 1950s. The section in question was the north-south route through a major metropolitan center. The east-west route was up and running, as was the loop around the city. But the north-south route had stopped in the center of the city. The project started in 1957 and had been stalled since 1973. If my colleague was unsuccessful, the project would be scrapped. By the time he was called, an army of lawyers had created a morass of litigation, with enough documents to fill a courthouse. Stakeholders included:

The U.S. Government

The U.S. Department of Transportation

The U.S. Environmental Protection Agency

The U.S. Department of Energy

The state government

The state Highway Department

The state Environmental Protection Agency

Three county governments

Six municipal governments

A class representing 400 property owners

A homeowners association

A historic preservation society

The Sierra Club

Nine contractors

Four municipal utilities

The level of hostility was high. Positions had been steeled by 20 years of impersonal litigation. In these situations, individuals lose their identity as people. They become faceless enemies with labels—plaintiffs, defendants, bleeding-heart environmentalists, or heartless developers. This one even pitted advocates of state sovereignty against the federal authorities of Washington, D.C.

Imagine some of the costs of the conflict:

Direct costs of all the litigation—lawyers and experts

Lost productivity—time people spent in conflict

Extra time on the road for commuters and commercial vehicles

Opportunity cost of all those involved

Emotional cost

Loss of community

My colleague's first action was to set up a meeting with detailed ground rules for participation. This meeting was to hear everyone's story—to allow them all to vent their current feelings, concerns, and what they hoped to achieve as an outcome. Full disclosure was the ground rule.

The second meeting was to hear proposals from each stakeholder about how he or she would take care of the concerns voiced by each of the other groups. This is called "walking in each other's shoes."

The third meeting asked stakeholders to role play their "enemies." By now the nameless and faceless parties were beginning to be real people with legitimate interests and concerns.

Predictably, by the fourth meeting the desire to take care of other stakeholders started to emerge. This enabled consensus on all of the major issues. A feeling of joy started to emerge in the meeting room. Everyone knew that they all could finally return to the real business of their lives: the productivity of their real work and personal source of fulfillment.

In this case, full disclosure provided the grist for people to work with. Until everything is on the table, no one is dealing with the entire situation. The story also illustrates that resolution involves breaking an old habit: instead of making sure your concerns are taken care of first, resolution incorporates the concerns of everyone. You must listen, understand, and honor others' concerns. Recognizing others' needs gets you what you want, and legitimizing others' concerns sets up the conditions in which others can take care of your concerns. That is an essential part of the foundation on which you construct resolution.

Once "their" concerns are seen as legitimate, they become your concerns too; because they are concerns of the situation, the solution will readily follow. This happens because you have people taking care of people, not people who have a position or people who want something. Taking care of others is natural for human beings.

A key to resolving the brothers' situation was a frank discussion of what each wanted to do. Full disclosure is the keystone on which resolution is constructed. The steps of the model get people talking.

Summary

Information is the raw material that leads to resolution. Holding information can lead only to mistrust and escalation of conflict. Full disclosure is evidence of a good faith effort to work together toward resolution.

Reflections

Has secrecy and withholding information ever helped you get what you want in the long run? Think of a situation in which you are currently involved. Stop sharing information and see what happens.

Chapter Thirteen

PRINCIPLE 9

Learning Throughout the Resolution Process

OLD PARADIGM	NEW PARADIGM
Winning	*Learning*

Do you have the patience to wait till your mud settles and the water is clear? Can you remain unmoving till the right action arises by itself?

—Lao Tzu

While focused on winning, you may not want to know or listen to the concerns of other people. Your objective is to convince everyone you are right, no matter what.

Listening Leads to Learning

The process of coming together to resolve a conflict, assuming commitment and the necessary attitude of resolution, is an exercise in group learning. Learning is a useful way to get rid of the ego-based ideas of winning, being right, fixing blame, or doing it the "right" way. Learning puts you in a mind-set of discovery, allowing you the luxury of "not knowing" the answers or the specific path that you will take. This process lets you discover, explore, and learn with everyone else what the best solution is. As the process unfolds, everyone is educating each other about his or her situation, learning what is needed to understand the bigger picture.

Think of a group coming together with a set of desired outcomes. Everyone holds key information. No one knows the answer. By keeping the dialogue open the group arrives at an agreement in principle. For example, in a partnership dispute, everyone wants a fair resolution so that all can get back to work. Through an open dialogue during which you learn about the others' particular concerns, you learn your way to what an effective resolution might look like. The same is true for spouses, unhappy consumers, even strikers. The "learning" perspective is the most important component of creating value and opportunity in the situations that life presents. Resolutionaries don't know the answers, but they do know that the longer you can suspend knowing, the more comprehensive and creative the resolution will be. Until you know, you keep listening and learning.

Listening to others, and paying careful attention to your sensing systems, enables you to "learn your way through" without knowing what the outcome will be. Because of the trust it requires, I am honored whenever people grace me with the request to assist them. It is essential to learn to trust your responses. Don't look for the quick fix in situations where you are not clear, because you will only have to retrace your steps. Have the courage to stay with your uncertainty until the clouds disappear and clarity is revealed.

In the two brothers' situation, no one knew what was going to happen. We educated each other in the process about needs and concerns. Eventually we all learned what we needed to design a satisfactory resolution. When you design a solution, it is important to check congruity with everyone as you go forward. The more the resolution incorporates the instruction of this feedback loop, the more satisfied everyone will be.

The Learning Boss

Masoud had been the plant manager for 17 of the 34 years that he had worked for a famous appliance manufacturer. Although he was respected by everyone, he was one of those authoritarian micromanagers who told you what to do. "My way or the highway" was the credo of his management style. This served him well for many years, but the young managers reporting to him who were responsible for operations were from a new generation.

Alice, one of Masoud's managers, had her own thoughts about the crew she supervised. In the area of work hours, she wanted to accommodate the child care concerns of both men and women. Masoud, however, believed the plant had three shifts, and that's when you punched your clock, period! Alice implemented some optional changes in shift schedules for her workers. The productivity improvements were immediate and significant. Alice was accurate that concerns about children detracted from the focus and enthusiasm her workers brought to the job.

Masoud found out what was going on. He was not pleased with Alice or with her initiative. Oblivious to the results, he focused on the violation of "his" rules. He sent a memo to all supervisors outlining his policy, intimating that anyone violating the rule would be terminated. He did not mention Alice by name.

Alice persisted. Although she had the support of the vice president of human resources, she did not want to play this trump card. Alice felt the tension grow between her and Masoud. It robbed her of time and energy for other productivity improvements.

Alice decided to resolve the matter. She had several goals in mind: (1) to gain Masoud's approval of staggered shifts, (2) to impress upon him the importance of listening to employees, and (3) to consider the unique situation everyone brings to the workplace. She asked to meet with Masoud.

With the skills of international diplomacy and the experience of 30 years as a wife and mother of six, she asked Masoud to think back to the time when his family was young. She had him step into his wife's shoes. She asked him to imagine how his wife might be less than fully present on the job if she was concerned about the welfare of their children. Alice also had Masoud think about how he would react as a father if he shared the responsibility for child care. Masoud started to see her point. She then pointed to the productivity increases. Reluctantly at first, but with growing enthusiasm, Masoud started to come around.

Masoud has become a plant hero. With Alice's help, he developed new work rules. Now employees create their own schedules. The productivity improvements and increased autonomy of plant workers have greatly impacted the way workers feel about their jobs. That translates into greater efficiency and reduced turnover and absenteeism. Out of the conflict, Masoud learned a great deal that contributed to his long-term effectiveness as a plant manager. If he had remained concerned about being right, he would have missed the lessons.

The Circle of Partnership

Carl and Mitchell decided to leave the safety of the large law firm in which they were partners. One Saturday they sat at the same computer terminal and filled in the blanks of a boiler-plate partnership agreement. They agreed to be the meanest lawyers their city had to offer.

They had both been through many battles about broken partnerships. They felt experienced enough to structure their own agreement. They addressed all of the legal details like monthly draws and sharing income, professional incorporation, termination, and what would happen in the event of their death. They even agreed how to divide files if they split up. What never entered their mind was what would happen if they developed philosophical differences about their work.

About three years into the partnership, Carl had a serious family tragedy. His 7-year-old daughter was killed by a hit-and-run driver. Most people expected that the incident would harden him, but it had the opposite effect. Carl lapsed into a period of introspection and reflection. He interpreted the death as a signal, a punishment, a wake-up call. Carl was sure this was the payback for all the hard-nosed lawyering he had been doing in the name of professionalism and being the best, which for him meant being the toughest.

During this time of introspection, he explored the field of mediation. He realized that in many situations he had not been providing value for his clients. Carl decided that mediation was a better way of resolving conflict. He started recommending this route to all of the firm's clients. Mitchell did not know what to do, so he started a lawsuit to stop Carl from speaking to their clients. Carl did not fight back. He called Mitchell and asked for a meeting. Mitchell refused, given that the matter was in litigation. A judge decided Carl could not be denied his interest in the partnership. By then the law firm had been destroyed.

Even after all the litigation, Carl wanted to have an ordinary conversation with Mitchell. Finally, Mitchell relented. Carl pointed out where an ordinary conversation would have taken them three years ago. He convinced Mitchell to review the situation through a different pair of eyes. He shared what he had seen all along. He put the hard-nosed advocacy into perspective, saying that it was valuable, but only for a narrow class of cases. Mitchell learned. They are partners again.

Summary

Creative resolution is an exercise in group learning. The longer you can stay in a place of "not knowing," the more comprehensive your solution will be. You must keep your mind open to learning facts, concerns, and perspectives of all people involved.

Reflections

Next time you have a situation of conflict, approach it as a learning exercise. See what you can learn about the situation. Notice how smart you can be!

Chapter Fourteen

PRINCIPLE 10
Becoming ResponseAble

OLD PARADIGM	NEW PARADIGM
Defer to Professionals	*Becoming ResponseAble*

Some people grow under responsibility, others merely swell.

—Hubbell

For many of us, some of the operating principles, paradigms, and systems of our culture dilute one of the unique experiences of being human—the privilege of self-consciousness. We have sanitized, professionalized, and diluted some of the interactions that can provide greater self-consciousness. Some of us have abdicated personal responsibility for our deepest individual concerns. We do this when we avoid conflict. We stay clear of direct contact with others by delegating to "professionals." We often do this before looking within ourselves for the answers. This is important because the more we know about who we are, the better we can collaborate with others.

There is a very important distinction here. Going to someone for guidance and education is profound. Looking for help is resourceful. Dropping the situation in someone's lap is not!

Taking Charge

You may deal with the challenges of conflict by giving it to professionals. You have been taught to believe they know how to do it right! That makes us a spectator in our own life, missing out on the discovery of our own internal and external resolutions, based on our personal standards. In resolving our own conflicts, we can find out who we are, our standards, and the substance we are made of. Under the new paradigm, you remain the captain. You become "responseAble." By this I mean that you deal with internal and external conflict. You get the direct experience of interacting with other people, human to human, without professionals doing it for you. You get to look at your own conflicts and collaborations. You get to be responsible for the quality of your life experience, instead of having someone dictate that quality based on their standards. On the other side, you don't get someone else to blame. That is little to give up for the gift you receive in return—the gift of *yourself* and the discovery of knowing more thoroughly what defines you.

The two brothers chose to be responsAble. Rather than abdicating to professionals and allowing a third party to decide for them, they took charge. They chose a form of assistance that helped them get to the core of their conflict. It wasn't pretty, it wasn't nice, it wasn't sanitized—but it was real, and they learned a great deal.

The brothers had the privilege of discovering their feelings, thoughts, reactions, and emotions as they stood toe to toe in a situation that confronted their life. What they learned about themselves would not likely have happened in another forum. Following the old paradigm, they would have been robbed of their life experience. I was proud that they seized the opportunity of learning more about who they were.

The Reluctant Father

A couple who had been divorced for five years was involved in a heated child custody and visitation dispute. They had two kids, aged 7 and 10. Mom was remarried, and her new husband had a great career opportunity located two states and a four-hour drive away. Mom was intent on moving out of state with their two children. Her former husband was intent on proving that Mom was wrong to leave, although his real concerns were not being mentioned. Dad never wanted the divorce, so the situation was an opportunity for him to play out his resentment.

The situation was very tense. Under state law, absent Dad's consent, Mom was required to get the court's permission to move. The opportunity for Mom's new husband would result in a significantly better lifestyle for the kids. They would be living very close to their maternal grandparents and to a school that would provide special programs for the older child, who was gifted. But Dad would not even talk about these benefits of a move.

The court battle reached a watershed when the kids were interviewed in the judge's chambers. They both expressed a desire to move. After that, Dad chose responseAbility despite his previous position. He heard the concerns of his children.

The experience of life as a human being is fraught with challenges. It always has been. Given food, shelter, and the absence of predators, our two primary challenges in terms of long-term survival are:

1. Civility—the ability to manage behavior that impacts others

2. Collaboration—the ability to work together.

Becoming responseAble is the key to meeting these challenges.

Summary

Deferring to professionals can steal your experience of finding out who you are. Your personal identity is revealed as you observe your responses in dealing directly with your own conflicts.

Reflections

Think of a time that you made a choice to defer to another person or professional. What were you feeling at the time? Were you frightened? What thoughts and emotions do you have about the outcome? Was it resolved to your satisfaction in terms of your emotions? How would you wish the outcome were different? Is there an unresolved situation going on in your life right now in which you are not being responsible? What actions could you take that would show greater responsibility on your part? What is the risk of not taking them?

Part IV

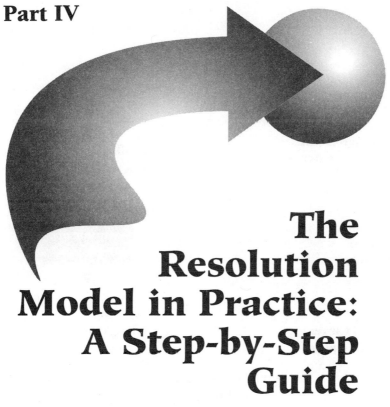

The Resolution Model in Practice: A Step-by-Step Guide

New behaviors are needed if you want improved results. Part IV details the seven steps of the Cycle of Resolution that leads to resolution. Each chapter discusses one of the steps, using case studies and explaining the dialogues that take you to resolution. Part IV concludes by showing the connection between the model and the ten principles of the new paradigm and showing applications of the model.

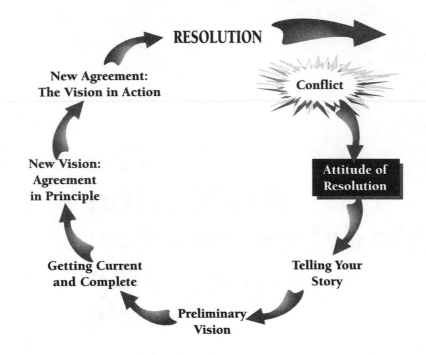

RESOLUTION

Conflict

New Agreement:
The Vision in Action

Attitude of
Resolution

New Vision:
Agreement
in Principle

Getting Current
and Complete

Preliminary
Vision

Telling Your
Story

Chapter Fifteen

STEP 1

The Attitude of Resolution

If we keep following the idea of an eye for an eye and a tooth for a tooth, we will end up with an eyeless and toothless world.

—*Gandhi*

The first step in the conflict resolution model is developing the attitude of resolution. This means choosing the new paradigm embodied in the ten principles. The attitude is developed by listening, sharing concerns in a situation, and knowing there is an agreement waiting to be discovered. The attitude of resolution is the opposite of thinking about winning or losing.

Initially, practice and conscious intention will be required to turn the new attitude into a new habit of thinking. To help you develop this new habit, this chapter discusses several skills to use and some obstacles to avoid.

Adopt an Attitude of Discovery

Embracing an attitude of resolution requires a perspective of discovery, as you engage in finding out more about another's point of view.

Through dialogue you understand what people want and what the situation requires. To stay in the discovering mode, you put aside thinking that you have the "right" answer, "know" what is fair, or have the "truth."

Take a difficult personal situation. Pretend you are not involved. Think about how it is impacting people you care about. From this vantage point you can reflect more clearly. Taking on the following behaviors will be very helpful:

1. Respect for everyone and his or her viewpoint.
2. Sincerity and open-mindedness in listening.
3. Integrity—trustworthiness and fairness.
4. Dignity and clarity that you will do well for everyone.
5. Authenticity and candor in communication.
6. Knowing you have *a path* to an answer,
   not *the* answer.
7. Confidence that the resolution will be discovered.
8. Centeredness when others lose their cool.
9. Humor and tranquillity.

Stepping into this way of being is not easy or simple. For this reason, this chapter discusses these behaviors at length. But if you are not sure how to exhibit these behaviors, I suggest you follow the advice that noted therapist Milton Erikson gave to a group of psychiatrists. Erikson told the group to "act" as if they knew what they were doing, until they discovered their own mastery.

Listen

I recently observed the resolution of an employee claim against a major financial institution. The complaint was based on racial and age discrimination and breaking an employment contract. The situation was resolved in three hours. The key ingredient: listening. Each side told its story in complete detail. The resolutionary listened with impeccable focus. Then he repeated to each person what they had said, almost verbatim. They knew he was listening.

Because everyone was heard in intimate detail, a high level of trust was established. Each side trusted that the resolutionary was their advocate and that their interests would be protected.

There is always common ground. I have come to understand that people, especially intimates, often are on the same side of a conflict. Unfortunately, our use of language in expressing what we feel and the expectation of opposition often prevent people from recognizing that there is no disagreement. Listening carefully and asking questions prevents useless conflict. You must listen with more than your ears. You must listen with your eyes and your sensitivity. You must always remember that you have one mouth with which to speak, but two ears to listen.

Maintain Your Commitment to Resolution

You must believe that resolution is just around the corner—that it will emerge from the next round of communication. The following story illustrates how the commitment to resolution "saved" the lives of a man, a woman, and an unborn child.

A colleague, Ron, was in a very difficult love relationship. His girl-friend Elyse became pregnant. Ron wanted her to have an abortion. Elyse was clear that she wanted the child, but because of the acrimony she was not interested in a long-term relationship with Ron. There were many possibilities for the couple, but none of the choices seemed satisfactory.

Elyse asked that he pay for the medical costs of the pregnancy and the birth of the child, nothing more. Ron agreed. But because Ron was not resolved about the choices they faced he wanted to do more, so during the pregnancy Ron provided little things like maternity clothes. As the months passed, he noticed his inner trouble deepening. Ron was pregnant too, even though the relationship did not seem viable.

About a month before the child was born, Ron honored his promises and made his last payment toward the medical expenses. As soon as he paid, he was served with a lawsuit for child support. He felt devastated and betrayed. He called me to scream, express outrage, and discuss his rights and possible actions. His legal rights were limited, so I suggested writing a letter to Elyse "telling his story." The letter arrived a few days before the birth. Elyse wasn't interested in what he had to say. This further inflamed him.

Ron and I strategized and communicated to Elyse and her attorney that if they changed the game and had Ron pay child support, he was going to be a father to his little girl. He did not do this out of anger but from his heart. Ron had been considering taking a larger role, and they had pushed him over the line. They declined our offer. Ron said that he would still honor the original agreement (pay medical expenses) or pay child support and be a father, but he would not be exploited.

I met with Elyse's attorney and spoke to her from a place of clarity and conviction of a vision for the future. Integrity emerged from my certainty about the best outcome. It seemed clear (my preliminary vision), given the relationship between Elyse and Ron, that everyone would be better off if the child was brought up by a single parent. The certainty with which I spoke to Elyse's attorney got through. She conferred with Elyse. They agreed to drop their demand for child support if Ron irrevocably surrendered all parental rights to the child.

Even this resolution produced an emotional dilemma for Ron. He had wanted a child, and briefly he had a daughter. I helped guide Ron through his personal agony. Outwardly I handled the legal questions, negotiations, and agreements. That was a small part of the work.

The real service was the attitude of resolution I brought to the situation—guiding Ron through conflict to a resolution of what he would do, given his choices and his emotions about those choices.

The choices had far less to do with anything outside himself—lawyers, lawsuits, money—than with his own values, beliefs, and emotions. Aside from the resolution, something very important happened for Ron. He had never felt so supported. He learned about the value of a guide who was committed to his well-being.

When you are facing a difficult situation, do not waiver in your belief that it will be resolved.

Sit Down and Talk

The way to resolve conflict and build relationships is through effective communication: plain talk about real concerns, not piecemeal sharing of information packaged for winning or to satisfy the requirements of a legal proceeding. When lawyers tell their clients to stop talking to the other side, they ensure no resolution until the legal proceedings take their course.

A corporate counsel for a Fortune 100 company has made starting a lawsuit an arduous task for his lawyers. The lawyers must first document that they have made an almost heroic effort to resolve the matter in the least invasive way. This process was put in place because it was often easier for a lawyer to file suit than to show the "weakness and vulnerability" of just talking to the other side. The internal documentation required to justify filing suit is more onerous than opening a dialogue with "the enemy." This company's practice contributes to resolution. The motivation is economy and efficiency. It works, and it conserves resources.

Have Fun!

It is important to have fun with an attitude of resolution. I do! Laugh at yourself as you disarm people committed to a fight. Watch their faces drop and their bodies relax when you listen and speak from a mood of resolution. Gandhi was right when he said that the British can't win if 80 million Indians won't fight. It works, even with the thorniest adversary. Prove to yourself that most people don't want to fight; it's a learned response.

A mood of civility leads to relationships that resolve things. When you declare that you want resolution, the mood of the dialogue shifts from a battle to a collaboration. Even if you're pretending at first, it will become effective. It will become real very quickly when you see the results.

I counsel clients to go directly to the source of the breakdown: the person they are fighting with. First I evaluate their attitude and do my best to engender a mood of resolution. I try to change their expectation about the outcome.

For example, Manuel was being threatened by his former company. They were headed to court to prevent his soliciting any of their clients. But Manuel was an independent contractor, and he had no employment contract restricting what he did. Meanwhile his old company owed him more than $20,000 in commissions.

Coaching him to hold a mood of resolution helped. Manuel received every dollar without litigation or further threat of any kind because he was able to approach the matter with a mood of resolution. You can have the same result. Think in terms of getting to resolution, not winning. Don't think about your position; think of a fair resolution for everyone.

Obstacles to Achieving an Attitude of Resolution

Working against your achieving an attitude of resolution are aspects of the old paradigm—legal standards, legal rights, and what is considered "truth."

Legal Standards

What participants in a conflict think is "fair" is a far more useful standard for resolution than what the law might dictate.

Recently the CEO of a multibillion dollar public utility paid $25 million in damages to an 8-year-old boy who was almost electrocuted. Despite his lawyer's advice that he was not legally responsible, the CEO felt that the right thing to do was make a quick payment. He was following a different standard. The following fable illustrates the point.

A Middle Eastern couple was having severe marital problems. Fatima wanted a divorce; Ali was torn by the conflict between his wife and his mother.

It was customary in the culture for a man to provide living quarters for his mother after his father died. Not only did the mother live with her son, she also got to pick her quarters. Ali's mother occupied the main floor apartment of a two-story house. The second story was occupied by Fatima and Ali. In order for Fatima to get to her quarters, she had to pass through her mother-in-law's apartment. Every time she did, she was berated for one reason or another. Her patience was exhausted.

Ali did not want to be disrespectful to his mother, and he did not want to lose his wife. He did not know what to do. Fatima and Ali went before the town elder and each told their story.

Fatima spoke of her frustration and anger; Ali spoke of being pulled in opposite directions by the two women he loved. After hearing both sides, the elder, with a twinkle in his eye, proposed a resolution. He suggested that they obtain a ladder so Fatima could enter her apartment without confronting her mother-in-law. It worked. That's resolution! No thought was wasted about who was right and who was wrong or what the legal standard was. The elder just designed a practical, effective solution.

A famous mediator shared his experience of returning to the family law firm after getting all A's at his first year of Harvard Law School. He was bragging to his uncle about his performance in contracts and criminal law when his 88-year-old grandfather asked him how he did in "settlements." As mentioned in the preface, the most effective attorneys know that resolution, not winning, is what's important.

Rights

Your "rights" are usually not the most important aspect of a situation. Emotion, past relationships, and future collaborations must be considered. Especially important is the kind of relationship you want in the future. Thinking only about "today" may not serve you.

If you know a situation will change, take that into account. In a recent divorce, I sensed my client would be in another relationship before too long. I suggested she accept a "discounted" one-time payment instead of periodic alimony payments that would be cut off if she remarried or lived with someone. This tack prevented a brewing battle about whether she would receive alimony for the rest of her life. Even though she had rights, it was smarter not to push them.

Truth

You probably think that the truth is very important. There are, however, many truths in every situation! Truth is usually elusive, sometimes irrelevant, and always dependent upon who's evaluating and their standard. I believe that people want the "more than truth" that resolution provides, because often everyone has a different "truth."

When I started practicing law, I believed there was "a truth" that you could find in the courtroom. I was representing a client who was injured in a motorcycle accident. He had one story about what had happened. The driver of the other vehicle had a different story. The eyewitnesses had another story, as did the investigating officer. After listening to the stories I was convinced each one was telling the truth. Everyone had a different picture. No one was lying. As I learned more "perception," I learned "a" truth about truth: everyone has his or her truth, and often there is no "the truth."

A magistrate was presented with a case of a contract to sell a house. He listened to the eloquent owner and said, "You're right." He listened to the equally impressive buyer and said, "You're right." When both sides confronted him with his inconsistency he said, "You're right." The "truth" doesn't always set you free!

When They Won't Cooperate

A question I am frequently asked in my workshops is how to achieve an attitude of resolution where people have dug in their heels, or they have a difficult personality, or they have more power in the situation than you have. This is a subject many people find challenging and frustrating. There are no easy answers, and sometimes people won't budge, but here are some suggestions that have worked for me:

1. Honor their position and their personality—make friends with them. Fighting and resisting will get you nowhere. When you push against a force, it will push back against you with greater intensity. Better to be empathetic and gain an understanding of where they are coming from and how they got to that place. Once you understand them, you can form a strategy to get them to the table.

2. Show them the cost of the current situation and the ongoing cost of no resolution. Use the cost of conflict analysis in Chapter 2 to demonstrate the ongoing enormous loss they are suffering.

3. Show them the potential benefit of the creative solution you have in mind. Let them see what they stand to gain.

4. Have the resolution show up as their idea. People sometimes resist an idea that is not theirs. If you lead them to where the idea becomes theirs, they buy in more easily.

5. Appeal to a higher authority. Is there someone with more influence than you to whom the resistant party will listen and honor, such as a boss, public official, legal provision, moral authority, or the like? You don't get a prize for doing it by yourself.

6. Ask yourself about whether you are seeing the situation from their perspective. In other words, are you out of line, and is their "unreasonableness" justified?

7. Don't give up, no matter what. The only way you get to

resolution is by taking the journey. Remember, sometimes the hardest part is getting them to the table.

Leadership and the Attitude of Resolution

When you choose an attitude of resolution, you implicitly become a leader. In your leadership roles, when dealing with differences at work and at home, it becomes up to you to keep moving toward resolution. Remember, the resolution model can be used by you as a professional resolver of conflict, as part of your job, with friends, or within a personal situation.

At work you might have a conflict with your boss, a member of your team, or people who report to you. You might resolve a conflict between two or more of your direct reports. At home you might speak to your wife about a conflict between your respective careers and the demands of running the house. At your church you might speak to other members about different values in selecting a new minister. An aspect of leadership is taking responsibility and getting the situation resolved to everyone's satisfaction.

As leaders you must be creative. Sometimes you wrestle with difficult situations for which there is no manual with the answers. No one said it was going to be easy, but holding an attitude of resolution helps a great deal. It is essential to develop and hold the attitude through all of the steps of the model.

Summary

The attitude you carry about conflict is a threshold that determines how easy it will be for you to accomplish what you desire. Listening and "learning" your way to the discovery and design of effective resolutions are essential skills. Paying too much attention to rights, legal standards, and "the truth" will often promote conflict. Adopting the attitude of "knowing" that a fair resolution can be found is a keystone for finding it. It can be as simple as an ordinary conversation, if you can let go of the need to be right and be willing to accept what is most effective for the future.

Reflections

Choose two situations of conflict in your life. Decide to take action in each of them. In one, try to prove that you are right; go for winning. In the other, take on the attitude of resolution and inquiry. How did they differ in outcome? In emotion? In terms of long-term relationships?

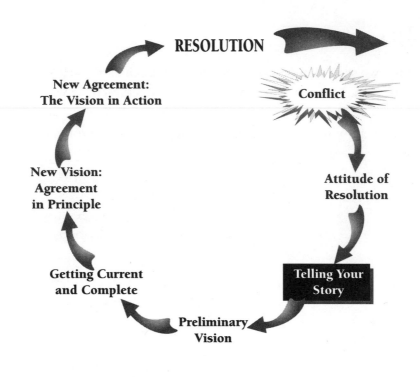

RESOLUTION

Conflict

New Agreement:
The Vision in Action

Attitude of
Resolution

New Vision:
Agreement
in Principle

Telling Your
Story

Getting Current
and Complete

Preliminary
Vision

Chapter Sixteen

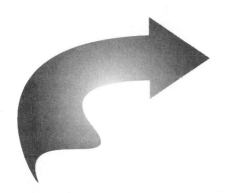

Telling Your Story

> When we haven't the time to listen to each other's stories we seek out experts to teach us how to live. The less time we spend together at the kitchen table, the more how-to books appear in the stores and on our bookshelves. . . . Because we have stopped listening to each other we may even have forgotten how to listen, stopped learning how to recognize meaning. . . .
>
> —Rachel Naomi Remen, M.D.[14]

We all want to tell "our" story. Reciting it, uninterrupted, to an engaged listener serves an essential, cathartic purpose. It is an important information-gathering vehicle for all concerned. This includes the storyteller, who learns from listening to his or her own story.

More Important Than Winning

My favorite illustration of the importance of telling the story comes from a lawyer in Canada. He had just finished a hearing before a judge. Although his client was with him, the matter was decided on legal theory and sworn affidavits; there was no need for his client to testify.

After two hours of the judge's reviewing exhibits, legal arguments, and hotly contested advocacy, my Canadian friend prevailed and won a $500,000 judgment for his client. He was very pleased and thought this a great victory. After the judge excused himself, my friend turned to his client and with an unusual display of effusiveness said, "Isn't that great? We just won half a million," to which his client replied with great disappointment, "But I never got to tell my story." The need to tell his story was as important as the financial victory.

We need to tell our stories. We need to have others hear our stories. Winning is not the only thing; it is not everything.

When you initially become involved in resolving a conflict, it is essential to listen to the story, the whole story, in the way the other person wants to tell it. Listen as if you were listening to a lover you do not want to lose who is threatening to leave. Make the other person feel that he or she has never been listened to before in the way you are listening now. Whether you are a participant or facilitator, remember that when someone tells his or her story, a change occurs for both the listener and the storyteller.

Professional Service

One arena in which it is essential to fully air stories is the establishment of a professional service relationship. Often the service providers do not get to the other person's real concerns because they listen to themselves and *their* notion of what's wrong or what needs to be done; or they listen through their professional filter and miss the full story. This is true whether it's a relationship with a therapist, physician, lawyer, accountant, consultant, contractor, auto mechanic, or home-repairperson.

When you listen to the full story at the beginning, you avoid a host of future difficulties, and you get much closer to providing exceptional customer service. Taking the time to let people fully air what is on their mind is a key ingredient in resolving their concerns and reaching their desired outcome.

Software Designers Who Told Their Story

George and Luke were software designers who had been working on the same project for seven years. George was a creative genius with broad-ranging design ability. Luke was an engineer by training and experience whose primary talent was his ability to keep plodding along. Each had a team of product developers whom they tried to inspire. George and Luke wanted to be role models for the people who worked for them.

Most of the time, when George and Luke worked together, things went smoothly. But during the last two years, George had decided that Luke's plodding style was hindering their creativity. He "knew" genius was demonstrated by intuitive flashes of brilliance and the epiphany of creative insight. At the same time, Luke became more firmly convinced that great leaps forward, although they sometimes had aspects of the intuitive, were essentially derived from the rigor of consistent application of principles and practices.

These stylistic differences made little difference until George and Luke were summoned by Maya, the CEO. She had just finished negotiating a make-or-break-the-company deal. Maya was not sure she could deliver on her promises. The desired results required a team effort. George and Luke would have to work in tandem. But they had no respect for each other! For two years they had spent each day in a private war. Now, their jobs and their company's survival were at stake.

Luke asked Jack, a senior human resources consultant, to help get them to the other side of their war. Although he held little hope of friendship and true collaboration, Luke saw a chance of developing a working relationship. Jack said he was up to the task, but he wanted to ruminate on the question of how to do it for a few days. Jack decided the only way to start down the path to resolution was to bring George and Luke together and have each tell his story. Since both of them respected Jack, a safe environment had been set up. In this situation there was nothing to lose.

As George and Luke recited their stories, each gained information, new respect, and appreciation for the other. Both were surprised to hear what the other thought about their approach to the work process. They listened eagerly as the other told his "truths," perceptions, observations, and predictions for the future.

Jack told George and Luke they would both be served if they suspended their judgments as much as they could. This was not a request to stop making judgments; that's part of our fabric and we all do it naturally. Rather, it was a request to "observe" the judgments and not take them too seriously. This is important, though it's not easy. Rather than defend yourself or make the other person wrong, listen so you can understand the other's reality.

When George and Luke returned to work, they had gained a new understanding of the other's capacity and competence. The genius of each person came through in his story. In sharing who they were, what they observed, and what they did, they put in place conditions for the best use of their talents. When it came time to make assignments for starting the project, George and Luke wasted no time in assigning themselves to what they did best and requesting help in areas where the other was brilliant. The more they worked together, the more respect they gained for each other.

The stories of Luke and George allowed each person to be heard and legitimized. How many times have you had an initial impression that shifted when you had a greater experience of someone? Please remember that.

The Manager Who Could Listen

In the early 1980s, shortly after the break-up of the Bell system, Jose found out that one of his salesmen, Shelly, was on a task force involved with a new telecommunications application. Jose was furious. He was never asked for his approval, and he did not think the application made economic sense. He called Shelly into his office and told him not have anything more to do with the task force.

Shelly was a self-confident independent thinker. He was not sure why Jose had taken the position he had, or what to do about it. Shelly did not like being told what to do, but instead of telling Jose "where to go," he decided to sleep on it. Shelly had chosen the project because he felt strongly about its economies of scale. He believed in the project and wanted to be a part of the implementation. He decided to participate, Jose's permission or not.

Early next morning Shelly went to Jose's office and told his story about why he wanted to be involved. He spoke about how the project made sense and why it was the wave of the future. The group Shelly wanted to join was pushing into new territory. The members would be "intrapreneurs," designing their own marketing, sales, and implementation material. They would be scavenging for needed resources. They would be out from under the bureaucracy.

Shelly convinced Jose that the potential rewards were worth the risks. He reached Jose's heart as he told a story from his own heart. Shelly revealed himself, and Jose favorably responded. Shelly's zeal was not misplaced. The project served as a model for corporate "intrapreneurial" action, and Shelly and his team were asked to train hundreds of managers in how they achieved their goals. Shelly learned the value of telling your story; Jose learned to listen!

Telling the Story of a Marriage

In marriage, the opportunity to tell the story is the opportunity to heal the breach. Coming clean, telling the truth, is the first step in the resolution. That's where healing begins. From your truth comes the authenticity that leads to new resolution.

A few years ago I was called into a situation everyone thought was hopeless. Jim and Irene had been married for five hard years. Each felt honor-bound to go the distance, no matter how difficult their day-to-day lives and no matter how the long-term prospects dulled the potential for an actualized life. Though their relationship did not work, they were more concerned with doing what they thought was the right thing than with doing what would make them happy. They each lived in a soulless shell compared to what was possible.

I was asked to see them under the guise of an ongoing disagreement about vacations. Irene wanted to go camping, and Jim wanted to stay at the Plaza in New York. I had brief conversations with each of them, and upon meeting them my intuition was confirmed. This couple did not want to be together, whatever the reason that kept the two living together. I say this knowing you can never understand what draws two people together, but this relationship looked like a mismatch.

My real service was to get them to talk about what was going on beneath the surface. I lanced the infection. I provided a buffer and an opening. The conversation took off. Each told a story of compromise, deprivation, and longing for a different, more authentic life. Because they were given a forum to tell their story, two lives were salvaged.

Kid Stuff

Rachel was having a difficult time with her 8-year-old. Ralph had been a model child. One day when Rachel picked him up at school, he got in the car, slammed the door, and said, "I hate that place!" Rachel started criticizing his conduct. This behavior went on for five straight days. On a few of those days, Rachel had screamed at Ralph and demanded that he change his behavior. He would not listen. Ralph was angry!

After consulting with her therapist friend, Rachel tried a new tactic. In a calm and reassuring voice she asked Ralph what was wrong and why he hated the place. Because of the opening Rachel provided, Ralph felt safe enough to speak. He told his story. Every day he was being teased by the boys in his class about the way he was dressed. The comments were creating a conflict. Because the comments were directed at the trousers that Rachel had selected, he feared that if he told Rachel the story, she would feel bad. It was easier to hate the place than deal with the conflict.

Rachel was thrilled to get the information from the story. It was easy to purchase different trousers. Listening to the story changed the outcome. Ralph no longer hates school. He no longer complains. He has stopped slamming doors. Telling and listening to stories goes a long way toward resolving difficulties you experience with kids. Children are people living within their own stories that must be honored and respected.

How often have you told yourself a story because it was easier than dealing with a difficult conflict?

Summary

The second step in resolving conflict is to listen carefully to all of the stories in the situation, including your own. Remember, listening benefits the other people involved as well as you, so let them have the experience of telling their story without interruption. Just because you don't respond does not mean you agree. At this stage your task is gathering information, and finding out the other person's reality about the situation.

Reflections

Most of us don't listen. We are waiting impatiently to speak or thinking about what we're going to say. To give yourself some insight into the value of listening, spend a day in silence, just listening to the stories in your surroundings. Put a sign around your neck saying, "I'm not speaking today, just listening!" You will be amazed at the connections you make and the value of the information you hear and observe that you usually miss.

Chapter Seventeen

Listening for a Preliminary Vision of Resolution

Only he who can see the invisible can do the impossible.

—*Frank L. Gaines*

Engaging in a process of resolution ignites sparks of creativity, and telling stories puts that creativity into play. The attitude of resolution illuminates a path on which resolution is discovered. The content of each side's story is the crucible that holds the potential for a solution honoring the concerns of all parties.

The potential resolution emerges in the same way that a "third body" is revealed when two individuals are in an intimate relationship. This third body has a viability of its own, born from the shared energy of all those involved. No individual can do this alone because each person has only his or her individual input. It's why talking to yourself about a difficult situation often leads nowhere; you keep spinning through the same thought process. The conflict needs to be viewed through a different lens. The alchemical fusion that takes place when stories are shared is both predictable and unpredictable.

You know it will lead to a resolution, but you don't know what the solution will be.

Whether you are a neutral third party (professional facilitator, friend, or manager) or one of the participants, as you listen to all the stories, you begin to sense the best solution. This requires detachment from any thoughts of winning or proving you are right. The visions of the future are the source of the new reality that is being designed. This vision attracts the energy and resources that will make it happen. This preliminary vision is the third step in the model of resolution.

In traditional wisdom among conflict resolution professionals, remaining neutral means not having a vision of the outcome; that vision is up to the people involved. However, try as you may not to, you will have a vision! Your mind will just do that. An effective resolutionary has a vision of the outcome, as participant or resolutionary. You must be careful, however, not to become too attached to your vision. As new facts, perceptions, concerns, and motivations are revealed, your vision of the resolution may change. Remember, your vision is not as important as their vision. But also remember, neutrality means being fair and impartial, not lacking involvement. Seek a balance.

Follow Your Instincts

The preliminary vision of resolution has its seed in feelings. The vision is intuitive, beyond the logic that will come later to justify it. It is the kernel around which a full resolution is formed, just as a pearl grows from a grain of sand. Our logical minds will find the rational basis to validate what our intuition and emotion already knows.

In this step of the model, faith and trust are very important. *Trust* is about listening to your deepest instincts. After you hear all the stories, you will likely have some undefined sense of where the situation might go. You get an idea of whether two business partners should stay together, whether a commercial relationship is viable, or what the best use of a city's resources would be. It is important to listen to that intuitive voice. It's not necessarily right, but it will provide a starting perspective that others can react to.

Faith is the faith to keep following your intuition even though you are not sure exactly why. The best-selling author Scott Peck says that when he was younger, he was often not sure of why he would do certain things or follow a certain path. He has learned to have faith and follow his instincts in the process. Eventually the logic and reasons are revealed.[15]

In the two brothers story in Chapter 3, I had a vision of brotherly cooperation. I held that vision as the process of resolution unfolded. Either brother could have held that position. Holding the vision as a beacon helped enable the result. I did not know the particular details, but I had a clear sense that resolution must include the perspective of brotherly cooperation. People in the midst of conflict usually are holding onto some past emotion. It may be up to a third person, or one of the participants who is ready to move into the future, to hold the new perspective.

Rick was a manic-depressive who had lost his fortune in the stock market mini-crash of 1987. He was ready to jump off a bridge. I sensed it was more important to deal with Rick's tenuous emotional state than with a lawsuit he would bring against his broker. I started painting a vision for the future: even if he recovered nothing in his lawsuit, it would be OK. I also had to deal with his vision of holding himself at fault—just more evidence of his own incompetence. I held a vision of his accepting the loss, doing what he could to recover financially, and forgiving himself for whatever he thought he did wrong. That came from trusting my intuition about a vision I had for the future.

Testing Your Intuition

Your intuition and feelings about the resolution are the starting point of a preliminary vision, a starting point from which you can test whether, and how, other pieces fit together. To test your preliminary vision and generate discussion about it among the participants, you can ask the following questions:

1. *Does the preliminary vision fit everyone's view of the outcome?* Find out early everyone's vision for the outcome.

2. *Does the preliminary vision take care of all specific concerns in the situation?* Everyone has important and unique concerns and interests that must be accommodated in the resolution.

3. *What needs correcting or adjusting?* In what ways is your vision off? How will the resolution need to shift to accommodate considerations you did not address? If anyone's vision is far from your preliminary vision, you may have to shift your expectation. You will have to understand other visions and begin the educational process that will enable everyone to understand the wisdom and benefits of different perspectives.

4. *What do others say about your preliminary vision's viability?* If you listen to others, you will find out all you need to know about whether your vision is workable. What they say will point to needed changes or to things they do not understand that must be explained.

5. *What concerns or fears does your preliminary vision bring up?* This is another way to find out what is missing from your vision. Because concerns or fears often stem from incomplete information, what further information must you provide to have others say "yes" to your projected outcome? Salespeople will understand this as "handling objections."

6. *What or who is missing?* The situation may call for pivotal additional information or the presence of a missing party. It is important to make sure that what is missing is brought into the situation.

7. *What must be learned or discovered to test your vision?* Is there some test that must be performed or a premise that must be validated? What needs to be set in motion to accomplish that? Perhaps the conflict is based on incorrect information.

8. *Is it a comfortable place from which to move forward?* Having shared your vision and listened to all that has been said to this point,

are you and all parties comfortable in moving forward? Are you ready to take the next steps knowing what you know? Are you confident you can reach resolution?

9. *Who else has suggestions or insights about anything anyone has said?* Even though you have a vision you think is brilliant, it is essential to listen and keep listening to the views and thoughts of others. As you hear what they say, you might learn something valuable because of the way they present information or because of your readiness to hear it. The important point is to stay in the inquiry for as long as you can.

Resolutions that I have helped facilitate as a lawyer, mediator, and consultant often came from a clear vision I had of the outcome. It was not an outcome that I wanted for myself; it was the outcome I thought was fair for everyone. That premise always guided my actions, and I was always ready to learn why it wasn't viable. Determining that viability is the purpose of asking the preceding questions.

Customer Focus

Sharon called Caleb with serious concerns about the computer system he had installed the week before. The system was designed to bring the 600-bed hospital into the 21st century. Caleb was the principal salesperson, and was also responsible for the installation. Caleb was the team leader with representatives from other departments of the manufacturer. Sharon was the hospital administrator. Right now the system was frustrating the hospital staff.

Caleb's worst fears were realized. For the past month, members of his team had been bickering. Each department knew that *its* way to install and repair the system was the *right* way. Units were not concerned with the system working, only with their own narrow sphere and with not being blamed for the problems. Even though Caleb held meetings to remind everyone that the hospital and patients' lives were the primary concern, Caleb's team members would not put aside their individual concerns to build consensus about the optimum way to proceed.

Although his job was at stake, Caleb felt compelled to call his division V.P., Scott Branch. Scott called all the unit heads that would be needed to fix the problems. Lives were at stake. The situation had to be fixed. Quickly! Within an hour the team was assembled. Caleb briefed Scott as they waited for everyone to arrive. Scott started the meeting by saying that his concern was the customer, their patients, and the business of saving lives and making people well. He held a vision of the system working efficiently. He acted as facilitator and motivator, never using his authority.

Scott spent some time clearing the air. He asked all participants to approach anyone they were angry with. The conversations that followed were not pleasant, but they were effective in getting everyone beyond their selfish frames of reference, lack of concern for other team members, and other departments.

Holding his vision of resolution, Scott attacked the multifaceted problem. He set up a procedure for evaluating each problem and choosing a plan of action. As each problem was presented, every team captain spoke to the problem and the best way to resolve it. They built consensus as to the best course of action. By now everyone was beyond his or her petty concerns and was focused on the customer. Everyone's "game" had shifted from being right to the creativity of discovering resolution.

By 1:00 a course of action was charted, and by 2:00, crews were in place implementing the plan. By 4:00 miracles started to happen. By 6:00 the system was under control, and by 8:00 everything was functioning within tolerable limits of the promised specifications. The source of the resolution was the clear vision Scott held of everything working well.

Aligning Vision and Expectations

My sister had just gone through a very difficult divorce after 20-plus years of marriage. As things started to get ugly, I wanted to help. I held the vision of a reasonable resolution. Being intimately involved with the situation and having seen the messy course a divorce can take, I was sure the situation could be resolved simply. I was wrong!

There was too much emotional baggage for the reasonable resolution I envisioned. That is not completely accurate: the ultimate resolution matched my vision, but their way of "getting to resolution" was much different from mine. They ended up going through a dozen court hearings, countless trips to the courthouse, and scores of telephone calls with lawyers.

It reminded me of what I had realized early in my career as a practicing attorney. In most situations you have a given set of facts and a defined context, which includes the controlling legal and environmental constraints. These are givens that do not change. To the facts and the context must be added a set of individual, personal expectations. Any professional has little impact on the context or the facts; these prescribe a predictable range of results. The area that can be influenced is people's expectations. I always tried to influence expectations because I knew that the difference between the expectation and the predictable range of outcome held the greatest potential for producing unhappiness.

As a mediator and consultant, I have always honored that reality. Getting the vision in line with expectations will always produce satisfaction.

Summary

A preliminary vision about the resolution will usually come up after everyone has a chance to tell his or her story. Trust your intuition that the vision that comes up is a good place to start a dialogue. If you are part of the conflict, make sure your vision contains everyone's concerns.

Reflections

Think of a situation that is bothering you. If you take into account the concerns of everyone in the situation by walking in everyone's shoes, what is your vision of a fair outcome? What do you need to do to make that vision a reality? Do it!

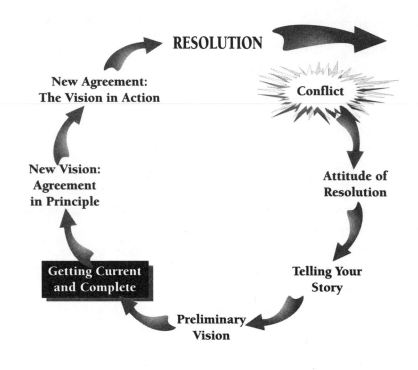

RESOLUTION

Conflict

New Agreement:
The Vision in Action

Attitude of
Resolution

New Vision:
Agreement
in Principle

Telling Your
Story

Getting Current
and Complete

Preliminary
Vision

Chapter Eighteen

STEP **4**

Getting Current and Complete

He that cannot forgive others, breaks the bridge over which he must pass himself; for every man has need to be forgiven.

—Lord Herbert

Getting Current and Complete is a pivotal step in the model of resolution. But before discussing the "how to" of the completion process, it is important to understand how it serves the process of resolution.[16]

Purposes of the Completion Process

Much is revealed by you and to you during the completion process, and a great deal happens internally that helps build consensus. Often you hold onto a preliminary vision because you believe a particular position is right. After the completion process, you may view the situation differently. When you understand that the others in the situation are not the enemy, that they likely want the same general outcome as you, and that their perspective and position is legitimate even though you may not agree with it, resolution becomes possible.

The completion process serves a number of very important purposes.

Disclosure

The primary purpose of disclosure is to ensure that everyone has disclosed all the information he or she has about the situation. The process extracts a complete picture, with all of the internal dialogue and attached emotional impact. In contrast to telling the story, the completion process involves asking specific questions designed to elicit feelings and emotions about the story.

In both business and personal situations, it is essential for all involved to participate authentically if they want to get to resolution. I make that request at the beginning. If people are not committed to being authentic, why waste everyone's time? People are often concerned, especially in business, that there may be adverse consequences from complete disclosure. But in a lawsuit, you are compelled to disclose everything as information is "discovered" by the other side. Completion works best when everyone understands that the benefits are worth the risk of vulnerability and disclosure. Otherwise, you waste productivity because of hidden, private motives.

Getting Current

The second purpose is revealed in the name of the step—completion. The past is brought current so you can move into the future. You have said all that can be said about the matter up to that moment in time. All internal chatter is out in the open. You declare that the matter is now behind you. Now you can design the specifics of the new agreement that will govern the relationship in the future.

The Alchemy of Emotion

Third, and most important, the questions of the completion process ensure that you go deeper into your feelings and emotions about the situation. The process provides a safe context for you to articulate things that are highly charged. During the completion process, the "alchemy" of resolution takes place. "The other's" concerns and vulnerability are fully revealed. You cross over a point on your internal continuum between the desire to be right and your sense of compassion about the situation. What surfaces is the natural human desire to take care of the concerns of a business partner, friend, colleague, or family member, even if you are presently in conflict. The shared emotion of vulnerability makes possible a new agreement and a new form of collaboration that can give you the benefit of your original expectation, if everyone can see that is still possible. It happens—between colleagues, business partners, and spouses. This process enables the internal work that is pivotal for reaching the next step in the process—an agreement in principle.

Letting Go

In the alchemy of emotions discussed above, the crossover to feeling compassion in the conflict is fostered by the attitude of resolution. When the third-party facilitator or the participant leading the completion process internalize the attitude of resolution by rising above personal concerns about winning and being right, everyone benefits. It's why the attitude of resolution embodied in the ten principles is so important.

In addition to being a participant, you may become a warrior—a champion for resolution. You have the wisdom and experience to see the resolution taking form, and you gently guide yourself and others to that place. If you stay open-minded, you can lead others to a resolution, even though it might not be exactly where you thought. Everyone is learning about the current status of the situation and his or her deepest feelings about it. The more authentic, open-hearted, and honest you can be as you reflect about what is said, the more satisfying the outcome.

Completion requires you to walk in their shoes. That is the key to getting to resolution. It overlays the completion process.

The Completion Process

What follows is a description of the process and the conversational steps that must take place. At each step, all parties speak until they have no more to say. It works best when done at a brisk pace, just saying what comes to mind, without filtering or trying to be nice. There is no discussion, just speaking and listening. Candor is essential. The intention is to experience a cleansing expression, a letting go.

Although I discuss the specific steps as though administered by a third-party facilitator, the process can be facilitated by a participant. The process also can be self-administered for use with internal conflict. For that I suggest you speak aloud so you can listen to what you are saying, or write it in a journal.

The steps in the completion process can be taken using two options. Option One is best suited for more intimate relationships (long-term partners, close colleagues, married couples, or family members) or when there is the desire or necessity of a continuing long-term relationship. Option Two is for more formal business environments. The statement and specific questions to be answered for each option are listed below, followed by explanatory material. The explanatory material can be told to the participants verbatim, or it can be paraphrased. After each question is answered, a "file" should be created in your mind that contains the conversation. That file can be "stored" or "deleted."

Option One—For Intimate or Ongoing Relationships

Statement. *If you are ready to envision a new agreement for your future relationship, it is important to bring your relationship current.*

It is essential for you to commit to the future and to fully participate in this process. The deeper, more vulnerable and authentic your
disclosures, the easier it will be to get to resolution. Listening carefully, to yourself and to others, is important. Understand that they live
in a different reality than you. What they say may not be "the truth,"
but it is *their* truth. Please don't respond or discuss what is being said.
Just speak or listen.

   1. *What worked about the relationship, partnership, or venture?*

You must say everything that worked about the relationship. This
will force you to reflect and remember better times—the aspects of
the relationship that were productive and satisfying. Your holding the
other person as an enemy dissipates when you focus on what worked.
You realize the value of the relationship that you once shared, and the
value of the "other."

   2. *What didn't work?*

It is important to hear what the other person says did not work. In
a reflective and quiet mood, start to become accountable for your participation in the breakdown. You will begin to see how you might
have done it differently, how your actions might have violated the
other person's standards and concerns, and what new actions you
might take. This is useful for the future of the relationship and for
your own growth and learning.

> *Somewhere in the next two steps, internal resolution will take
> place! Anger and righteousness cannot occupy the same space as
> forgiveness and gratitude! You will have to work very hard to re-
> sist resolution.*

   3. *Who do you need to forgive and for what?*

The purpose of this section is to get you to let go of the anger you
are holding. Forgiving others, and yourself, enables you to let go of
what you have tied up in the past. You are then free to move into the
future. Just saying the words doesn't make it so, but the declaration is
an excellent beginning.

4. Who do you need to thank and for what?

This part of the process enables you to go through the breakdown and get into honoring and legitimizing others. It forces you to see the value others have brought. It's hard to hold onto your anger and blame when you step into a mood of gratitude for what they did. All should both forgive and thank themselves!

5. What else do you need to say so that you are complete enough to say, "Today is a good day to die"?

This is a catchall that provides the opportunity to say anything that has not been said. It is part of the Lakota "warrior blessing" ritual. Before a war party set out, the holy man would ask each warrior if it was a good day for the warrior to die. If he could reply "Yes," he was in a warrior state and ready to move forward without distractions.

6. Do you have any requests?

This serves two purposes. Essential matters that may need immediate attention can be addressed, making this the beginning of new coordination. Second, the new requests put you back in action with others, demonstrating that no matter how bad it was, your common humanity allows you to take care of present concerns and prevent further deterioration and loss. In the two brothers' story, there were requests made about sharing information in customer files so business could continue.

7. Declare that the conflict is current in the moment and complete! You must say it!

The declaration that the conflict is in the past serves a powerful purpose. You can now be present with each other with an opportunity to design the future. Of course there will be a residual of past feelings, emotions, and beliefs that only time will quiet, but you have made the matter history by the power of your own declaration. You have made a commitment to a more useful perspective.

8. What's the new era? The new era is _____.

This gives you the opportunity to name the new era and declare what your future relationship will be. From a broad statement of intention about what the new relationship will be come the specifics that go in your new agreement.

Option Two—All Other Situations

This is a more businesslike way of asking questions very similar to those in Option One. The same explanatory notes apply.

1. What was effective about the original agreement? What worked?

2. What was ineffective? What didn't work?

3. What can you say by way of compassion for the other participants' shortcomings or incompetence? (forgiveness)

4. What can you say by way of respect for the other people, their competence, their contribution, and their conduct in the situation? (thanks)

5. Pretending for a moment that you will never have another opportunity to speak about this matter, what else do you want to say?

6. Do you have any requests?

7. Declare completion!

8. What's the new era?

The Completion Process at Work

During the process of completion, the two brothers opened a window to each other's heart and mind. Forgiveness and respect emerged. It was forged from airing the residue of what had broken down. That residue provided the raw material for the fabric of a new partnership. It was a different bond, forged and tempered from the heat of adversity and the cooling salve of catharsis and communication.

This is a sacred process. It is a great honor to be a guide and witness for people in relationships that have broken down. I am awed by what can emerge when people are committed enough to open their hearts, forgive, and let go of the past. Here are some stories that illustrate its effectiveness.

Completion Within a Partnership

Moriah and Bob were partners. They had pulled their consulting company up by the bootstraps. It was poised to move them into national recognition because of their innovative work in developing human potential. Their clients—individuals and companies—loved them and their work. But they were human! In their relationship, their personal psychological patterns were surfacing. They were resenting each other. They had stopped communicating. What seemed to be a great business marriage was turning into a nightmare. The atmosphere in their office was affecting their work, their income, and the future of their business.

They reached a point in their relationship where they had to clear the air—either move forward with a new level of understanding, or separate their professional lives. They were familiar with the completion process. I suggested that they go off alone one afternoon and clear the air. Their conversation would not be easy—hard work and emotional honesty were called for. But through their tears they emerged as a stronger partnership. They learned they had the same vision for the future. They realized that what was setting them off was not what the other was doing but their reactions to their own "ghosts" from the past.

The courage to have a "real-time" conversation put their collaboration back on firm ground. They designed a new foundation for their working relationship based on current truth. They agreed to do "a completion process" every six months, no matter how well things were going. Today their partnership thrives. Each time they get complete, they free their creativity to go to the next level.

The breakdown of relationships that happened with Moriah and Bob occurs in all business and personal relationships. What we perceive in the external world is a reflection of all of our previous experiences. Often we are not aware of how much impact this has on our present "reality." But our past is the source of most conflicts.

Completion Within a High-Tech Company

A few years ago, I introduced the "technology" of resolution to the executive committee of a growing technology company. The committee members were convinced that they could conserve a great deal of productive energy if they knew how to deal with conflict. The executives became fascinated with the entire process. They adopted the completion process as part of standard management practice. Now all teams, and every reporting relationship, come together four times a year to make sure nothing that could detract from productivity is unsaid.

Completion Within a Family

Jerry and Lenore were locked in combat—to be right, to maintain control, to win, to get their way. Life was awful, even though they loved each other deeply. What unfolded was far better than the most riveting movie I have ever seen. I witnessed two people move from a great anger to great compassion. As they talked about what worked in their relationship, they realized the contribution they had made to each other. When they spoke of forgiveness, they forgave themselves for being angry, and not seeing the way they had been jerks. They forgave the other for their anger.

When they looked at thankfulness, they realized the value they had created—two great kids, a home, a circle of friends, and a business that employed 20 people. Their anger melted into love, and their fear turned to possibility as they decided to reinvent their relationship. Today they are thriving, both as a couple and as business partners. They emerged from the completion process with the ability to tap into the fun, humor, and creative genius that brought them together. They tapped the source of their original attraction.

Completion Within My Family

Last year, I decided to reframe my relationship with my parents. As is the nature of the parent-child relationship, I was carrying around the baggage of how my life was tarnished by their parenting. Mostly, they have been fine parents, always doing the best they could at the time. Going through the completion process was not easy, but it was very satisfying. It provided a sense of freedom most people don't get until their parents are gone. It completed the part of the parental relationship that locked me into the struggle that is part of parenting dynamics. It allowed a shift to a foundation based on common interests. I freed them of the need to be caretakers. I gained emotional autonomy.

Summary

Bringing everyone into the present moment is an essential component of resolution. The completion process ensures vulnerability about a situation. The structured conversation reveals feelings, empties emotional background, and moves you to stand in the other's shoes. It reveals the loss and the disappointment over expectations that are unrealized. It provides a context in which people grieve, let go of the past, and start designing the future.

Reflections

Practice the completion process three times: once with yourself about some part of your life you want to change; once with someone in your family; and once with someone at work. What was the value for you? For them? For the next three days, do completions about anything that troubles you. Notice the change in your attitude.

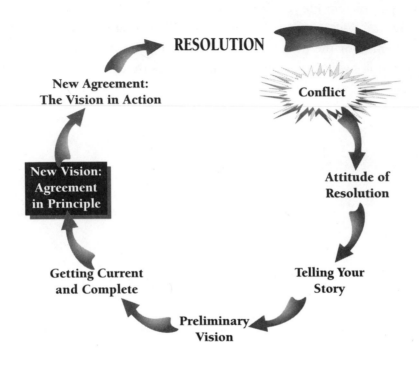

RESOLUTION

New Agreement:
The Vision in Action

Conflict

New Vision:
Agreement
in Principle

Attitude of
Resolution

Getting Current
and Complete

Telling Your
Story

Preliminary
Vision

Chapter Nineteen

Reaching Agreement in Principle

If men would consider not so much wherein they differ, as wherein they agree, there would be far less of uncharitableness and angry feeling in the world.

—Addison

It's happened hundreds of times. One side of the anticipated battle calls, fearing the worst—thinking of hiding assets, who will win, who will lose, and what will be the consequences of a battle. They are amazed to discover that aside from the emotion of transition, the process can be relatively painless. Once you establish an agreement in principle, it can be easy.

By developing an agreement in principle, a broad brush understanding of the resolution, you sustain the momentum generated by the completion process.

Some questions for everyone to reflect on that will help sustain the movement toward an agreement are:

1. After the completion process, is the preliminary vision still on target?

2. How does the preliminary vision have to be modified to get to an agreement in principle?

3. Is the preliminary vision history? Do you have to start fresh, based on what has been articulated in the completion process?

This chapter discusses several techniques for answering these questions, which moves the process to an agreement in principle.

Trial Balloons

Telling the story and the completion process provide a clearer sense of where the situation is headed. Now you can use some "trial balloons" to see if you have a foundation for a new agreement. After the completion process, generate a discussion by asking questions about concerns like:

Companies—Are there business reasons for working together?

Colleagues—Will they continue working together?

Partnerships—Will we continue to be business partners?

Executives—Do they have a basis for a joint vision?

Litigation—Do we want to settle the claim or go to court?

Employment claims—Does an employee want to retain his or her job?

Divorce—Is there a desire for fighting or peaceful resolution?

A slight variation to using a trial balloon is making a suggestion. The phrase "what do you think about the idea of . . . " works well. It opens up the discussion by throwing a ball out. Others are free to pick it up, and the responses will give you ideas about where everyone is in the process. The opening gets everyone designing the solution.

Small, Bite-Size Chunks

Securing agreements in principle is best accomplished by taking small chunks within a context that "nothing is agreed until it is all agreed."

Most people are less uptight about signing off on a particular concern if it is not written in stone. This provides leverage in the situation with which you can bargain. In business disputes the keystone inquiry is whether, or how, people can continue working together. In a divorce, I like to establish early who will have child custody, a basic understanding about property division, and whether there will be a claim for alimony.

Group Dynamics and Difficult People

In the conversations among participants as you move toward an agreement in principle, remember that group dynamics are involved. People need to get comfortable working with each other in a new way. Folks have different levels of awareness and interpersonal and intrapersonal skills. Posturing may happen at the beginning. Even with good intentions and similar desired outcomes, group and personal dynamics are factors with which you must deal. People sometimes need to get beyond their insecurity and fear. It can be helpful to air these feelings as a preliminary to the entire resolution process, rather than waiting until the agreement-in-principle step.

There will be difficult personalities. They will come in a variety of shapes and sizes. Stay aware of hostility and the forms in which it manifests: indecisiveness, complaining, negativism, silence, arrogance, and agreeableness. There is a body of knowledge and information for you to access in dealing with difficult facets of human personality.[17] Consult it when your common sense has not worked.

The Irresistibility Principle

The irresistibility principle is a good way to get to an agreement in principle. In almost every conflict or new project, you can frame the desired outcome in a way that people in the situation will find irresistible; they have to say "yes." A good illustration is the irresistible frame that my ex-wife placed around our divorce settlement. At the time this happened, we were both actively practicing lawyers. I was starting to get "lawyerlike" in the situation regarding our divorce settlement, and one day she called and said: "We have been through too much together, our friendship is too important, and to have anything but an honorable outcome would demean the marriage and our relationship. Let's agree that we will do this as friends, and preserve the dignity of what we have shared."

Light bulbs went off. It was irresistible to go for this result; on reflection it was the obvious way to move forward. Unfortunately, most people, because they have no model of a better way, choose what they think is standard—a battle.

The two brothers had two irresistible outcomes—brotherhood and no battle. Earlier in their conflict, no one had raised the concerns of preserving family. Often the essential part of resolution is reframing the perceived problem into something else. Asking people to look back from their "deathbed" is a good way to get into the discussion. Ask what they would like to see as the way they resolved the situation and how they would like to feel about themselves because of it. That is a very useful tool.

Ongoing Feasibility Testing

Continuous feasibility testing is an important aspect of getting to resolution. Constantly check to see if everyone is engaged and on board. Poll for both major and minor objections. This keeps you on the path. Just keep asking!

There is No "Right Way"

Are you concerned about making sure you do it right? You will! When you multiply the number of conflicts with the number of people who want an effective agreement, you have the number of right ways to accomplish this work. Being good at achieving desired outcomes is about having a positive intention and trusting your instincts. The right way is the way you sense will work. Often you just have to "feel" your way along. The conflict resolution model is the foundation from which you will develop your own artistry. You were born with most of the skills you need!

Relief and Excitement

An important barometer in this step of the model is whether you are relieved and excited about reaching an agreement in principle. Moving from an agreement in principle to a complete agreement is more businesslike than the emotionally taxing work done up until now. The key hurdle is getting an agreement in principle after doing the deeper emotional work. When you have a basic agreement, you can breathe more easily. You are now on the same team. This is what the completion process is designed to accomplish.

It's a joy to observe an agreement in principle being reached. People realize they will not have to fight. I have seen the tension leave the faces of joint venture partners, business partners, unhappy consumers, fighting spouses, battling neighbors, executive teams, and companies and their employees. It confirms that even though we have trained and girded ourselves for battle, we don't want to fight.

Summary

An agreement in principle is an elegant way to turn the corner and is a big step toward reaching agreement. It's like being at the top of a ski run. From there you slide to the bottom, but you must steer along the way. The key is reaching agreement on broad understandings and framing things in ways that make them irresistible.

Reflections

Practice the irresistibility principle by looking at a few situations you see as difficult. What suggestion can you make that everyone, including yourself, will say "yes" to? Introduce what you think will be irresistible by asking, "What do you think about . . . ?"

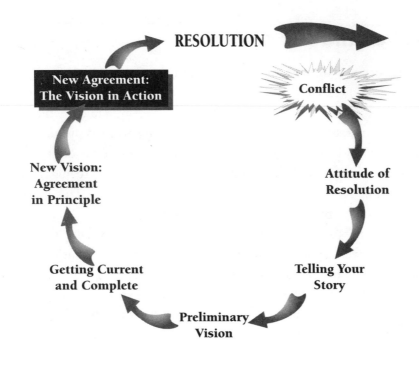

RESOLUTION

Conflict

New Agreement:
The Vision in Action

Attitude of
Resolution

New Vision:
Agreement
in Principle

Telling Your
Story

Getting Current
and Complete

Preliminary
Vision

Chapter Twenty

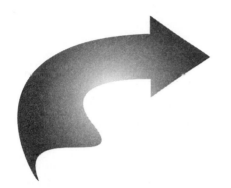

Crafting the New Agreement

Covenantal relationships induce freedom not paralysis. A covenantal relationship rests on shared commitment to ideas, to issues, to values, to goals. . . . Words such as love, warmth, personal chemistry are certainly pertinent. Covenantal relationships are open to influence.

—Max DePree, Leadership Is an Art[18]

Resolution is present when you have a shared vision for the future. What was intolerable becomes history. Because the conflict is no longer present in your life, you no longer think about it. In the agreement step of the resolution model, you articulate the innovative solutions that you and the others in the conflict invent together. It puts the meat on the bones of the agreement in principle. In the process, this creates trust which eliminates conflict or, in the case of a new relationship, facilitates starting on a solid foundation. How to reach an agreement—the sixth step of the resolution model—is the subject of this chapter.

The Power of Agreement

When you think about agreements, you probably think of difficult negotiations and long legal documents. You focus on protecting yourself from the "what ifs" of the situation. A more useful way to define *agreement* is as: (1) a joint vision; (2) the product of an effective conflict resolution process; or (3) the foundation for a successful new team, partnership, or relationship.

This definition is true for your business or domestic partner, spouse, family members, colleagues, work teams, or joint venturers or for your company and its employees or customers.

Agreements define how you coordinate the activities of people working together—how they collaborate—and collaboration is the foundation of any accomplishment. Successful collaboration is like dancing, but often you have different ideas about the steps in the dance. These differences can lead to greater synergy or to breakdown. Creating synergy and excellent results depend on clear agreements. Effective agreements express joint vision, a road map for producing results. The art of crafting effective agreements increases the likelihood of obtaining desired outcomes.

The Laws of Agreement: Why Agreements Are Important

The following laws of agreement explain in a linear way why agreements are so fundamental to work and to life and why they are the foundation for coordination, the essence of productivity.

THE BAD NEWS	THE GOOD NEWS
You were not taught to craft effective agreements. It was not part of your core educational curriculum.	*You can learn!*

1. The source of productivity and fulfillment in any relationship is effective coordination. The tighter the coordination, the better the results.

2. You coordinate in language by making implicit agreements (talking to yourself about what you think the agreement is)

and explicit agreements (discussing the agreement with others).

3. You work and live in a "sea" of agreements.

4. You never learned the essential elements of an effective agreement.

5. Clear agreements express shared vision and how to get there. Clear agreements empower and contribute to desired results.

6. Clear agreements improve the chances for satisfaction. They set up the conditions that produce delighted clients, customers, teammates, colleagues, vendors, and family members.

7. Practice enables you to craft masterful agreements.

8. No matter how clear and complete the agreement, everything will not be addressed—conflicts and differences will arise.

9. Breakdowns are not a cause for alarm, they are to be expected. Breakdowns are an opportunity for creativity.

10. Resolving conflicts leads to new agreements.

Mastering the Art of Agreement

Each of the following elements is an essential part of an effective agreement. Use these elements as a template for constructing agreements. If you discover other elements or think of a better way to articulate them, please let me know. What makes an effective agreement is a work in progress.

It is useful to reach an understanding about each element with the others in the process; this process is very important because it is the beginning of a new working relationship.

The elements of an effective agreement are as follows:

1. *Intent*—The big picture of what you intend to accomplish together must be specified. The first step of any effective collaboration is sharing a big picture of what you are doing together. This provides a framework to hang the details on.

2. *Specific vision*—A joint enterprise works best when everyone is working toward the same specific goals. The clearer the detail of desired outcomes, the more likely you will attain them as visualized.

3. *Roles*—The duties, responsibilities, and commitment of everyone must be clearly defined.

4. *Necessary parties*—Everyone necessary to achieve the desired results must be part of the agreement.

5. *Promises/commitments to action*—The agreement contains clear promises so everyone knows who will do what. When commitments to take action are specific, you can determine if the actions are sufficient to obtain the desired results and what actions are missing.

6. *Time*—All promises must have specific time deadlines for task completion. These are "by whens"—by when will you do this, and by when will you do that. In addition, the time period the agreement will be in force must be specified.

7. *Value of exchange*—This specifies who gets what for what. Is the exchange satisfactory? Is it fair? Does it provide adequate incentive? This must be clearly understood, and everyone must be satisfied or someone will sabotage the transaction.

8. *Measurements of satisfaction*—The evidence that everyone has achieved his or her objectives must be clear, direct, and measurable so there can be no disagreement. This element is critical because it eliminates conflict about the ultimate question—Did you accomplish what you set out to do?

9. *Concerns and fears*—Bringing unspoken difficulties to the surface provides the opportunity to anticipate and minimize the disagreements you know will happen during the collaboration. The discussion will deepen the partnership being created or let you know this is not a partnership you want to be part of.

10. *Renegotiation*—No matter how optimistic and clear you are, it will become necessary to renegotiate promises and conditions of satisfaction. Circumstances change, and you must put in place a mechanism to address the new conditions. Being realistic about this at the beginning enables the relationship to evolve and prosper.

11. *Dissolution*—It is imperative to provide everyone with a way out—an exit strategy everyone can follow with dignity. Anyone who feels imprisoned in a transaction, partnership, or relationship will not make his or her maximum contribution to the enterprise.

12. *Consequences*—Although you may not want to police the agreement, it is important to agree on consequences for anyone who breaks a promise.

13. *Dispute resolution*—Acknowledge that conflicts and disagreements arise as a matter of course as people work together. If you know that and establish the attitude of resolution and a process that leads to a new agreement, resolving conflicts will be easier.

14. *Management*—Someone must take responsibility for stewarding the project and ensuring the agreement is honored and the intended results are obtained. While this is everyone's responsibility, it is important enough to have a point person.

15. *Agreement*—Everyone is satisfied and ready to take action. Work on the agreement until you are satisfied that you have an agreement or do not have one. Unless and until you are satisfied, do not move into action. You will not have a shared vision to work toward.

16. *Fun* Commit to embrace the future as a new opportunity that can be enjoyed. This attitude lubricates the collaboration. Laughter makes enjoyable what is sometimes an unforgiving world. If you can't see how the collaboration will be enjoyable, why get involved?

Three Phases of Agreement

As you learn to work with the elements of agreements, remember these three distinct phases:

1. *The process of agreement:* This is the series of conversations in which you talk about each of the elements. Following the process enables you to determine if shared vision and trust are present. If present, you can declare that you have an agreement.

2. *The phenomenon of agreement:* When you have completed the agreement process, you should have a shared vision. If you do, hearts and minds are together in a covenantal relationship focused on producing a certain result. If this phenomenon of agreement is present, you have an agreement that you can trust. If you do not trust that this phenomenon is present, you are not ready to move forward with the relationship.

3. *The artifact of agreement:* When you have the phenomenon of agreement, the essence of the covenant should be put in writing. This will act as a guide as you move forward with the relationship.

Agreements in Lieu of Conflict

The two brothers are a classic example of how the process works. When they agreed to a resolution, an agreement was crafted that expressed a new working relationship: Tom would own the existing business, and he would pay Bill for his share of that business; Bill would have exclusive rights to a geographical area in which to operate his new business; and they would help and advise each other so each could benefit from the experience of the other. They let go of their acute discomfort and pain. Each stepped into the new context that each had articulated for his future, demonstrating that the real resolution of conflict is a new agreement for the future.

A resolution between IBM and Fujitsu demonstrates how creativity can produce new value where others see conflict. Fujitsu had developed a computer operating system for IBM, which IBM wanted to use in certain applications. A dispute developed about ownership rights. Because of the possibility for thousands of individual lawsuits, litigation had the potential to keep an army of lawyers busy for decades. An agreement was reached that provided for preservation of the relationship through a series of cross licensing agreements. Instead of acrimony, both companies earned millions from their new agreement.

In another resolution, a bankrupt manufacturer who owed over $1 million to a former supplier induced the supplier to continue business in the future; in a new agreement, the manufacturer paid a premium on future supplies to cover the past debt. It enabled the supplier to get whole eventually, and the manufacturer to emerge from bankruptcy, regain viability, and save the jobs of thousands of employees.

New agreements are especially important for divorces that involve children. It is fortunate when parents understand that co-parenting gives children the benefit of two parents and that children will be harmed if acrimony continues. Working out the details of co-parenting is the first step in a new form of collabor-ation.

When you step into the new paradigm, you will not have to "process" the conflict. You will not be concerned about fixing blame, inducing guilt, or being right. You will not have to suffer. You will realize that joy and productivity comes from coordinating with others and that the "dance" of agreement is the edge where life is rich and exciting. You want to be back in action quickly. Just put in place new agreements and move forward. The conflict will be in the past, superseded by the new agreement. That is my vision.

Agreement making is a practice that can be learned and mastered. Try it! I guarantee your results will improve.

Summary

Crafting effective agreements is an elegant way of arriving at a shared vision for the future, either as the final step of resolving conflict or as the initial step at the beginning of a new project, transaction, or relationship. It is an essential skill that you never learned. The laws of agreement provide a simple logic that demonstrates the value of agreement in any situation. By using the elements of agreement you achieve the "phenomenon" of agreement, a relationship based on covenant.

Reflections

Choose someone you admire, someone with whom you want to work on a project. Approach the person and, using the agreement template, craft an agreement about the project. Try it at home—work out an agreement about an area that has been troublesome, and watch the conflict fade into history.

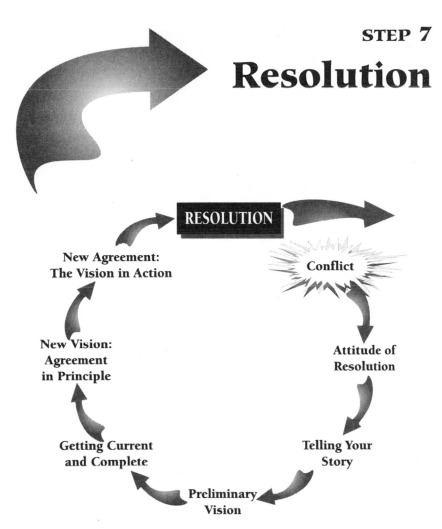

Chapter Twenty-One

STEP 7

Resolution

Resolution is . . .

Resolution is an outcome.

Resolution is the condition of everyone and each one's resources after a conflict, dispute, disagreement, or breakdown is put to rest.

Resolution induces everyone to address his or her relationships.

Resolution returns everyone to productivity and coordination.

Resolution requires:

- Moving from conflict to a workable agreement, a dynamic context for action and cooperation.
- Honoring everyone's concerns.
- Taking actions that put the conflict and its impact to rest.
- Committing to ongoing relationships.
- Getting beyond everyone's emotional positions.
- Establishing a vision for the future that lets go of blame, punishment, and damages and recognizes others' value.
- Recognizing new practices essential for the success of ongoing relationships.
- Being willing to learn and having the courage to change and the compassion to forgive.

Masterful resolution requires that all involved say:

- They have won.
- Their resources have been optimized by the process.
- Although conflict and breakdowns are inevitable in life, they are in better condition to handle them in the future.

This chapter discusses how to manifest the vision the resolution embodies.

Manifesting Your Desired Results

Scientists in quantum physics labs have observed that certain subatomic particles exist only when they are observed. You might conclude that the power of observation, the focused attention of the conscious mind, has the power to create matter in the physical universe. Do we all have the power to think things into existence? This phenomenon is mentioned in the books of the best-selling author and physician Dr. Deepak Chopra.[19]

A correlate of this premise is that when you have a clear picture of what you desire in the future, the resources needed to realize the vision will be attracted to the situation by the power of your subconscious mind. This has been explained by Napoleon Hill in the classic *Think and Grow Rich*[20] and by Dr. Maxwell Maltz in *Psycho-Cybernetics.*[21]

Every principle, practice, model, and story in this book has one central purpose: freeing you to have the results and fulfillment you want with the least struggle and the most elegant use of resources. This is called *manifestation.*

The Laws of Manifestation

The following is a linear expression of the best way to manifest your vision.

1. Thoughts manifest themselves in physical form.
2. Consciously and habitually feed your mind thoughts that express the reality in which you want to live.
3. Express your vision in your thoughts.
4. Be very specific in your vision of the future.
5. Agreements are powerful tools of manifestation, expressing joint vision, producing synergy, and increasing value.
6. Agreements help produce satisfaction and material desires.
7. Consciousness about our thoughts makes us human.
8. You can choose what you think!
9. See Law 1!

The Importance of Clarity and Specificity

Since your thoughts and visions become real in the physical universe, the best way to explain the importance of a specific vision is with a favorite story.

Amy was in the depths of despair over the pending bankruptcy of her once-booming auto dealership. She was about to end it all. She went to the beach for a last moment of solace and communion with nature. She became fixated on a glass bottle of other-worldly shape. The bottle, with a radiant glow, washed to the shore and she picked it up. Given her impending death, she felt no fear as she reached over and pulled the cork. To her great surprise a large beautiful genie emerged from the confines of the bottle.

When she asked, "Who are you?" the genie bellowed that she had been sent as a gift from the forces of "goodness" because of the exemplary life Amy had led. The genie would grant any wish on the condition that Amy remain alive. Amy thought for a minute and, although skeptical, agreed to the conditions. The genie asked for her wish. She replied that her vision was to have a successful foreign car dealership in a major city. The genie said that when Amy woke up, her vision would be reality.

As she drifted off to sleep, Amy was still quite skeptical but figured she had nothing to lose. She went to bed with thoughts of Hondas in San Francisco, Toyotas in Miami, BMWs in New York, Mercedes-Benzes in Denver. . . . Upon waking she found that the genie was true to her word. Amy was in Istanbul, with a thriving Ford dealership. She learned the importance of being specific about your vision!

Resolution Is Leadership

Over the past few years I have worked with three models of leadership that specify a number of leadership behaviors. The characteristics of these models are parallel to the principles and behaviors this book discusses.[22, 23, 24]

A few years ago I asked nationally known leadership expert Jim Kouzes "When do leaders give up, change directions, or realize they have been barking up the wrong tree?" Without hesitation he said, "They don't. They don't blame others, they don't make excuses for poor performance, they don't quit. Once they decide on a course of action, they just keep moving forward, making corrections as they go along, but not turning back."

This same tenacity gets you to resolution because resolution embodies the same competencies and behaviors essential for effective leadership. You must understand, honor, and be thankful for the different values and realities that everyone brings to a situation. You give yourself the authority to resolve things so that action and productivity will proceed. You continually define ambiguity as a situation unfolds so that you form a context of relative certainty. You develop a compelling vision for the future that gives purpose and meaning to the tasks of others. Acting like a resolutionary contributes to your personal identity as a leader. It will be recognized by people working with you because it is a hallmark of leadership.

Summary

Physical reality is shaped by your thoughts. Combining your thoughts with those of others to produce shared vision is a powerful leadership tool that contributes to producing the outcomes you want. This is achieved through the power and principles of manifestation and resolution. At the end of a conflict, or the beginning of a new project, there is great power in the resolution that a clear, shared agreement has produced. Leadership is taking responsibility for making things happen in the world, and the same characteristics that make excellent leaders make excellent resolutionaries.

Reflections

Think about something you have been wanting in your life. Choose someone to partner with in making it happen. Craft an agreement with that person. Notice the resources that arrive to support your vision. Do this at work and at home.

Chapter Twenty-Two

How the Resolution Model Applies the Principles

If we work in marble, it will perish; if we work upon brass, time will efface it; if we rear temples, they will crumble into dust; but if we work upon immortal minds and instill into them just principles, we are then engraving upon tablets which no time will efface, but will brighten and brighten to all eternity.

—Daniel Webster

Following a model to resolve conflicts and construct agreements for your projects, transactions, and relationships seems like a stretch because we are reluctant to talk in a linear way about things that we believe exist in a more emotional realm. This reaction reflects our habits of thinking. Most of us hold conflict as a "life force" and are afraid that eliminating the "drama" of conflict will take away a great deal of what drives us and makes us feel alive.

I am not suggesting eliminating the differences, only offering a new way of dealing with them—developing a new habit. Having disagreements and differences adds vibrancy to life, but ongoing, hostile conflict does not. Using the model will quiet your internal chatter and provide the freedom to be more productive in the present moment. Conflict and differences will not disappear, but you will respond more productively.

The model is an effective way of developing a new habit because, like a road map, it tells you exactly where to go—something that is especially important when you are going somewhere for the first time. It prescribes a series of steps that require using the principles of the new paradigm. To make clear how the principles and model connect, this chapter explains how the model serves each of the ten principles.

The Ten Principles as Applied to the Model

Abundance

This principle permeates everything. The model demands believing that there is enough for everyone to be satisfied. The principle of abundance is thus a foundation of the model.

Efficiency

The model takes the guesswork and wasted energy out of forming effective agreements and resolving conflict quickly. It provides a map that helps you:

1. Decide if you have a workable agreement.
2. Maximize the potential for success by creating a shared vision.
3. Minimize conflict due to misunderstanding.
4. Deal with conflict directly, at its core.

Chapter 20 discussed the key elements of effective agreements. The following discussion shows how these elements contribute to the efficient use of resources.

Intent and Specific Vision. With intent and a specific vision, you quickly begin thinking about the result you want—the big picture of the resolution or collaboration, as well as a specific picture of what you want to create together. You quickly see if everyone has the same vision.

Roles and Promises. When roles and promises are articulated, you know at an early stage whether these roles and promises are enough to manifest the vision, whether other people need to be brought in, and whether you can embrace your role.

Measurements of Satisfaction. If you state up front how the outcome will be measured, there is little wasted energy discussing whether you achieved your purpose. It is a yes/no observation—either you did it, or not!

Concerns and Fears. Concerns and fears are a huge drag on productivity, and speaking about them efficiently gets rid of this heavy baggage.

Renegotiation, Dissolution, and Dispute Resolution. Setting up a process on the front end for resolving inevitable conflict saves a great deal of emotional energy when these situations occur, and it contributes to developing the attitude of resolution.

Creativity

Creativity involves two important aspects. The first is emotional. Where conflict exists, fear is present, and fear is a great impediment to creativity. By promoting resolution, the model also promotes creativity. The other aspect is the value of structure. A model provides a framework within which you know and trust that the process will take care of the required elements; you won't miss anything. This gives you the freedom to be creative.

Fostering Resolution

Three elements of our present system guarantee conflict: (1) the adversary mind-set generated by fear of losing or of being taken advantage of, (2) the paradigm of cutting off communication once conflict occurs, and (3) the gamelike sport of win or lose that we take for granted.

Following the model eliminates these practices. The attitude of resolution recognizes that everyone loses when people respond to conflict in an adversarial way. The model is designed to get to resolution quickly and use conflict creatively. The model demands engagement and dialogue, which fosters productivity. Knowing that the process holds the potential for everyone to win takes away the jousting that is currently so prevalent.

Vulnerability

The model requires you to be vulnerable and authentic. The steps to resolution are designed to help you disclose your observations, reveal your feelings, understanding the grief arising from the disappointed expectation, and stand in the shoes of the other side. This requires authentic self-revelation. Revealing what the model requires—thankfulness, forgiveness, apology, and fears—demands vulnerability. The benefit is that agreements are formed, and transactions take place, much closer to people's core. The closer to "bedrock" the personal commitment is, the greater the potential result because of the depth of connection. You develop "relationships based on covenant."

Long-Term Collaborations

The agreement template builds long-term partnership. If you take the time to engage in conversations covering the elements of the agreement, you are serious about building something that will last.

The model is designed to articulate the joint vision. It is intended for people who are concerned about producing results and effective collaboration. Taking time to articulate a vision that incorporates the desires of all people involved is not a casual matter. Clearly expressing conditions of satisfaction provides long-term goals for the collaboration.

Feelings and Intuition

Using the model requires going beyond the rational and the linear. In going through the elements of agreement, you realize that the "phenomenon" or "covenant" of agreement exists—your heart says "yes." The "yes" comes from your entire self, not just your logic. It is much more than an intellectual exercise. Sharing fears demands attention to your emotions. So does grieving, and expressing thankfulness and forgiveness. The entire experience takes you beyond the left brain.

Full Disclosure

Following the model requires complete disclosure—at the beginning, when the relationship is first established, and as an ongoing commitment to keep the relationship clean (no internal chatter). When secrets are eliminated, the energy wasted on keeping them is available for productivity. You never have to worry about what you are hiding because nothing is hidden.

Learning

When you are resolving a conflict or structuring a new project, you are learning your way to the desired result. First, you listen and learn what others need. Then, you learn what you need. Finally, together you learn your way to the agreement that will satisfy everyone. A mind-set of inquiry rather than of "knowing" makes resolution possible.

ResponseAbility

You cannot leave it to a professional. You cannot hide behind a process that requires less than authenticity, engagement, and full participation. No one can participate in the practices of the model for you. You must be present in the agreement making discussions. You must decide if this is a person you want to engage and work with, a person who you trust to work through inevitable conflicts with you.

Summary

The principles are the foundation on which the new paradigm is based. Understanding how the model serves the principles will help motivate you to honor the principles and use the model.

Reflections

It takes approximately 21 days of repetition to "install" a new habit. So please either photocopy the list of principles or copy the principles on an index card. Carry the card with you and for the next 21 days, and before you sit down to eat a meal, review and reflect on them. Do not spend more than three minutes. The learning process will be helped if you share what you are doing with others.

Chapter Twenty-Three

Benefits and Uses of the Resolution Model

Nothing in this world is so good as usefulness.

—B.C. Forbes

You will find that the model is useful in all areas of your life. Remember, it's not brilliant insights that catalyze improvement; it's consistent application of simple principles. As you go through this chapter, please think about how using the model might improve areas of your life.

The Power of Resolution

A solid agreement embodies a clearly defined, shared vision of the future. It fuels productive energy forward, toward creating—manifesting—that vision in the physical world. The vision is the starting point of the creation.

The extraordinary freeing of energy that takes place when people realize they can put down their guns, take a deep breath, and get back to their productive lives is amazing to behold. Resolution confirms the human inclination to nurture, love, and take care of each other. This principle was illustrated by Chilean biologist and writer Humberto Maturana, who points out that the human hand is constructed in a way that is uniquely capable of caressing any part of the body. If you doubt the premise, imagine caressing someone with a hoof or a claw![25, 26]

I repeatedly observe the phenomenon of nurturance with business partners, executives, and divorcing couples. When the completion process is finished, the cobwebs are cleared. The individuals remember their attraction and harmony and can start working on an agreement as partners: they finish it in a fraction of the time expected, with joy and emotional release instead of pain. The weight of preoccupation holding down their productivity, growth, and the rest of their life is released. People have told me that it feels as if their wings have been restored. They feel light and unbridled, free again to soar. They expected a long, contentious, painful process. They did not believe resolution was possible.

The vice-president of marketing for a large manufacturing company was being "restructured" out of a merged organization. Even though he was not unhappy with his severance package, he was ready to fight for more. This stance was based more on what well-meaning friends were saying than on what he wanted. Rather than asking for a lot and getting involved in an extended conflict, he asked for a few things, which were granted, and he was elated. He could now turn to face the rest of his life. He did not have to fight about something in the past. His energy and creativity were free to devote to a new plan. This phenomenon was present for the two brothers from Chapter 3. Instead of a battle, they were building new businesses.

Imagine what the Hatfields and McCoys might have produced if they weren't always engaged in a battle. The same is true for the Bosnians and Serbs. The habit of "the life force of having an enemy" keeps you wasting precious energy fighting. The battles evidence fear—fear of an unknown future, a new order of things, and a new life force without an enemy to battle. You are holding onto an old structure because of the fear of not knowing what the new structure will be. You don't realize that you hold the power to make up the new structure. You can construct a future using the tool of agreement. This new agreement will be the new structure, although it is one you are not ready to trust. You have to learn that usually there is no enemy if you don't create one.

Incremental Power

There is great power in the resolution of joining your vision with others. The synergy of teamwork is extraordinary. Simple proof are the powerful Clydesdale horses that pull the Budweiser wagon. One Clydesdale can pull 7,000 lbs.; two can pull between 18,000 and 25,000 lbs. At a time when we all are being asked to produce more with less, we need greater incremental performance (accomplishing more with less) both at home and at work.

At work you are facing downsizing, rightsizing, reengineering, layoffs, and mergers. At home you feel increasing demands for personal growth; self-actualization; and being better parents, siblings, spouses, children, producers, or performers. You never feel adequate. The weight on your shoulders is dizzying. Each day you see the signs of fissures in the armor of the rugged-individual, Marlboro-man philosophy and culture that built the United States. How can you accomplish more with less?

Tight coordination and a shared vision allow the miracles of teamwork to occur. Clear agreement with others builds teams that can experience an exponential expansion of power.

Agreements at Work

Business is the central focus of capitalist society. It is a place where you participate as owner, boss, employee, and consumer. As you work with others in pursuit of common goals, opportunity abounds for resolving conflict and reaching clear agreements.

For example, agreements by senior executive teams create joint vision for the direction of an organization. They define roles, responsibilities, tasks, and how results are to be measured. The conversations leading to the agreement, and the action in pursuit of agreed-upon goals, creates covenant and collaboration. Companies waste energy as internal chatter clutters productive capacity. But when the model is followed, nothing is left unsaid. Get rid of chatter and you double your output.

Following are specific ways that clear agreements help at work.

Conflict Resolution. A conflict resolution process provides the peace of knowing that a path to resolution has been established. People can invent a new framework for their future. Nonadversarial ways of bringing closure to emotional relationships leave fewer scars and better soil for new beginnings with people you must work with.

Joint Ventures and Mergers. The level of success increases because detailed joint vision is articulated. Increasingly, business alliances with other organizations are used to build "virtual organizations." Agreements are also successful in incorporating departments of different companies into effective operational units.

Employment Relationships. Dr. Steven Covey says that to have empowered employees you need trust, and to achieve trust you need performance agreements.[27] The agreement spells out desired results, guidelines, accountability, and consequences. In effect, employees design their jobs. When people participate in shaping and customizing their working relationships, productivity leaps take place because the participants are inspired and motivated by the objectives and standards that they shaped. Mutuality is fostered, resentment is eliminated, and acceptance is assured.

Teams. Managers, department heads, and team leaders can use agreements to keep their units on the same track. Articulating a shared vision and establishing clear conditions of satisfaction are crucial to this task. They operate both within and between departments and companies.

This is also true for self-directed work teams, increasingly the backbone of business organizations. As you ask for increased participation and self-management, you must provide the tools that optimize team resources and keep everyone on track. Agreements, and the means to establish and revise them, are very useful, sorely needed tools. There are dozens of situations where team agreements are the "bible," used to evaluate performance and results and provide direction and guidance in implementing the organizational mission and specific team objectives.

Mood and Attitude. When you are engaged in designing the specifics of your participation, you are a willing player—less resentful, happier, and more engaged.

Productivity of Work Groups. The work becomes primary, not the "politics" of relationships. Joint vision and the tactical moves to achieve objectives become the focus. Internal chatter is quieted.

Creativity and Innovation. The absence of hostile conflict enables clear thinking which is essential to doing tasks more efficiently. The energy that was locked in conflict is available for creativity.

Consultants, Professionals, Vendors, and Salespeople. There is greater ability to build relationships that increase the potential of satisfying customers by crafting clear agreements that (1) establish a joint vision of desired results and (2) specify how the satisfaction of expectations will be measured. Clear agreements will make all vendors and service providers an integral part of the team because everyone understands his or her contribution to profitability and the satisfaction of the final consumer.

Customer/Client Satisfaction. When you are clear about tasks and free of chatter, you can concentrate on the customer.

Labor Relations. Unions become part of the team—partners in producing results, part of the virtual organization.

Legal Agreements. Lawyers can craft agreements that focus as much on achieving results as on protecting clients from problems.

Lawsuits. An early process that fosters resolution prevents situations from getting out of hand.

Diversity Issues. People see how they are the same and that they want the same things. Differences are acknowledged in the process of crafting agreements. As individual concerns are expressed and heard, people are "legitimized." Groups get the benefit of individual genius.

I consulted with a start-up technology company that was developing a new telecommunications application. The company had been stuck for six months. Marketing and product development were battling over ready dates; finance was breathing down everyone's neck; and the venture capitalists hovered over everything. In one day, we broke through and jump-started the operation. Developing clear promises of action and a joint mission got everyone moving.

I recently read Tom Petzinger's column in the *Wall Street Journal* that talks about self-organization.[28] As companies are flattened and new principles of management pervade, there must be a vehicle that people use to accomplish the work of the organization. The model of resolution can be that vehicle![29]

Agreements at Home

You don't think of having specific behavioral agreements with spouses, children, friends, or family members. I suggest you might find great benefit in rethinking your thinking. My experience is that agreements defining relationships can produce the quality we want in these personal situations and can help us reduce the source of friction.

In marriages and other intimate relationships, agreements can reflect unique individual realities. You can agree about areas of permanent concern such as relatives, social life, money, and career. Spouses can articulate what they want and need in their relationship. Family members can define what "family" means to them. Couples about to marry can design a customized foundation for the future.

There is as much value in the conversations that lead to the agreement as in the agreement itself. The model provides the structure for the conversations that explore individual thinking about a particular subject. It is a tool for deepening relationships and providing guidelines for behavior. Updating the agreement keeps relationships fresh and shifts difficulties from defensive explanations about behavior that have a psychological orientation, to those that are practical and behavioral. The model provides a means of resolving conflict without the need of outside help.

I used the model in a long-term relationship. My partner and I jointly produced a vision for the relationship that we wanted. It expressed our separate visions for the future and the vision we had of what the relationship would be. We made promises to each other about how we would act as a couple and how we would structure our lives. We placed a time limit on the agreement and had a structure for renegotiating our promises.

We included standards for the following areas of our life:[30]

physical fitness	family
finances	planetary concerns
play time	work
membership	spirituality
social life	education
personal dignity	career

The conversations that led to our agreements were extraordinary. Writing the agreement was an exhilarating exercise of joint creation, much more profound and stretching than either of us imagined. The agreement was a heroic document whose words were a powerful, inspiring force.

After five years we realized that we were not being served by staying together. Although separating was emotionally difficult, it was a smooth and orderly transition. The decision to separate, although painful, was not hard to make. When we evaluated the results that we had produced against the standards that we agreed on, it provided a clear answer about what we had to do.

As I look back, I am grateful for the experience. The inspiration and motivation provided by both going through the process leading to the agreement and living within the structure of the agreement were profound. The agreement was a catalyst for many of my accomplishments. It provided a foundation for the relationship, a foundation

I jointly designed. It was a personal banner far more empowering than implicitly adopting standards and norms that are accepted as part of our culture, which is what most people do when they get married.

A few years ago I was asked to help a family with a "rebellious" 14-year-old. I had never used the model in this kind of situation, but I saw no reason that it wouldn't work.

John was having difficulty in almost every area of his life. His grades were below expectations, threatening his ability to get into college. He was abusing alcohol and drugs. He was not showing up for school. He fought with his parents every day. Previous interventions included counseling with the school psychologist, private counseling, special summer camp, and every kind of punishment you can imagine. These were all attempts to fix someone who was not broken.

I invited the family for a session. The key to making the session effective was getting John to believe that he would be listened to without interruption, that he would be heard, and that his feelings and vision would be considered in the resolution. Once he believed that and he felt free to communicate, the process was not difficult. John opened with his anger and resentment about always being compared to his sister, who was seven years older. She was one of those perfect kids—straight A's, prom queen, president of her class, etc.

He didn't want to be her. He never felt "heard" in his desire to pursue theater and the arts. As long as his talents were not recognized, he would continue being defiant. It was his way of getting attention.

I asked John to articulate how he wanted to be treated and why. His parents were amazed at how intelligent and sentient he was. Together they crafted an agreement that provided detailed guidance about his education, contributions to the household, ability to make decisions for himself, and choice of friends.

He completed high school and started taking art courses. He enrolled in the local junior college while working as a draftsman for a local architect. He finished junior college near the top of his class, transferred, and will soon receive a degree in architecture. A key was legitimizing him by listening, and empowering him to participate in making up his future.

Agreements in Your Communities

Agreements can be used for mapping the direction and purpose of any organization. A few years ago, I was active with a self-appointed civic group that took up the banner of "reinventing" local government.

We used the agreement model to chart a course of action. The purpose of our group was to eliminate duplication of police, fire, road, vehicle maintenance, and parks and recreation services provided by municipalities, utilities, and county government, as well as to take advantage of economies of scale. We developed a vision of the desired result. It included a political referendum to fold all of the municipalities into one county government with continued representation from the formerly independent entities. This would eliminate waste and inefficiency.

Our agreement included a plan for gathering information, projecting potential savings, garnering political support, dealing with resistance, and engaging in political action. We made promises about what we would do. We had a series of expectations with time frames to let us know if we were reaching our objectives. We determined how to resolve conflict and who would be responsible for making sure that we were on track. Even though everyone wanted to move immediately into action, the up-front planning was worth the effort. It produced commitment.

Agreements can get to the real task instead of dissipating resources in an adversarial political process. About 20 years ago a community group was formed to build a school for autistic children. The school served as a statewide model for other local groups that were concerned with the same problem. To me, it is a classic example, worth telling here, of what coordinated action driven by passionate concern can produce.

When my law partner introduced me to the situation, the community group requested starting a lawsuit against the federal, state, county, and local governments and their educational and mental health agencies. The group consisted of the parents of 22 autistic children of varying ages. These children had slipped through the cracks of various federal and state laws; the bottom line was that no one would take responsibility for educating the children.

I suggested a slightly different tack. I met with a group of parents to determine what the parents really wanted. Predictably, their concern was giving their kids the best education, given the state of the art of dealing with autism. They believed starting a school was best. The kids were not mentally ill but severely emotionally compromised. We mapped out a short-term strategy for getting funds for the coming school year until a longer term resolution was put in place.

We had two strategies: (1) a legislative and fund-raising agenda and (2) starting a school. The parents were as committed and dedicated a group as I have ever worked with. Given the PR potential, their cause fell on receptive political ears, and they received approval and funding for a new school. Three years after that initial meeting, other school districts from the state were sending students to the school. This school was the first of a number that were funded around the state. That part of the story provides small gratification compared with the more important result. The dedicated school staff, along with outside experts, developed a program that was returning kids to the public schools. This was a result that was way beyond expectation.

Given downsizing and the need for more efficiency in government, the vehicle of agreement is a natural. As part of Vice President Gore's "reinventing government" program, I have reviewed agreements between President Clinton and the cabinet secretary's defining specific objectives for essential government departments. Although much more detail could be placed in the documents, it was evident that senior administration officials had embraced the idea of using agreements as a way to get things done. Bravo!

Agreements With Yourself

The model can be used to resolve intrapersonal conflicts or for planning—making agreements with yourself that chart a new course of action for your future.

George was having great difficulty with his ex-wife, Marsha. There was ongoing conflict surrounding their joint custody agreement. They had been through years of counseling before their divorce. They had been in and out of court and had spent thousands on legal fees. Finally, George realized he was a big part of the problem because he automatically reacted to the position Marsha took; whatever Marsha said, George said the opposite. I had a sense that if he sat down with the agreement template and made all the decisions without the input of others, it would help get him to the bottom of things. Shortly thereafter, when his pain was so great because he was afraid he might lose the joint custody arrangement if he couldn't learn how to manage himself, George sat down in the privacy of his room. Alone, he saw the whole situation. He realized that a new agreement with himself about his behavior (the only thing he could control) might be the end of the war with Marsha.

George's vision was their ability to have calm and purposeful parenting discussions in which he listened and tried to understand her motivations. He wanted his child to have the benefit of a co-parenting relationship. Discussions might then lead to consensus that incorporated their joint wisdom.

He made these promises to himself:

1. To listen to her.

2. To keep his tone conversational when speaking.

3. To take classes in communication skills.

4. To tell her when he was losing control so they could take a time out.

5. To apologize whenever he "lost it."

6. To penalize himself $100 when he broke his promises.

To measure whether he had met the agreement, he set a condition: going one full year without arguing with Marsha or calling his attorney. He acknowledged that no matter how resolute, he might not be able to pull it off.

But George was able to keep the agreement because it was voluntary; he had a different attitude than when his ex-wife, his lawyer, his therapist, or a judge told him what his agreement would be. At the end of the year, he was thankful, especially because of the long-term impact on his son Randy. Instead of living in the emotional tug of war between his parents, Randy is becoming the product of their combined wisdom.

You can use the agreement model to plan objectives and help get what you want. I use the model for setting goals about writing, income, and physical exercise. It works! Something happens when you exercise the discipline of crafting an agreement with yourself. Getting specific about your goals is a form of creative visualization. Anyone in the business of goal-setting will tell you that it is essential to write down your goals. Making an agreement with yourself is another form of doing that.

Summary

Having agreements for all aspects of our life seems radical; however, the effect is worth it when you examine the results produced in business, community, and personal situations.

Reflections

Spend one day looking at your life through the "lens" of agreement. Look at all of the relationships that you have and notice the implicit and explicit agreements that guide your actions. Think about the areas in which greater clarity would add to your personal peace and contribute to desired results. Choose two or three situations, and, using the models in this book, craft new agreements. Reflect on the process, and any changes in the productivity or satisfaction of the relationships.

Part V

When You Need Professional Help

*Part V shows how the model
for conflict resolution relates
to other methods of resolving conflict
and shows what to look for
if you need professional help.
It explains the value
of the legal system and
details the role model
of the resolutionary.*

Chapter Twenty-Four

Using the Power of the Legal System

> *It is to law that men owe justice and liberty. It is this salutary organ of the will of all which establishes in civil rights the natural equality between men.*
>
> —*Rousseau*

This book provides a model you can use to resolve conflict and avoid the high cost of professionals. Unfortunately, everyone does not aspire to the resolutionary standards advocated in this book. Fortunately, we have a system in place for people unwilling to engage in a peaceful process of resolution: the civil court system. The system has the teeth to make sure people honor its decisions. It enforces by coercive power. Our legal system provides a foundation, leverage, and a place of last resort. The legal system tells people what their new agreement is.

Because they protect against exploitation, the presence of the civil court system and its powers of enforcement hold the heart of liberty. As discussed in earlier chapters, the system is far from perfect and is subject to abuses in its application, but it surely does protect human rights. The subject of this chapter is how our legal system complements the model for conflict resolution.

Available Options—
Choices on the Continuum

The many dispute resolution services—including those that are part of the legal system—form a continuum. It is important for all consumers of these services to understand where their options are on the continuum. Although "professionals" might blanch at my simplicity, I'll summarize these options from the least to the most invasive.

Talking—It doesn't have a fancy name, but it often works simply and elegantly, as demonstrated in the model for resolving conflict.

Creative design—The least invasive and most empowering, creative design takes place when two or more parties sit side by side, looking at their "joint" problem with a mind-set of "how can we best resolve this situation."

Negotiation—Negotiation is a bit more formal, but in some ways it is not different from talking. We negotiate all day, in many different situations. But in our culture, negotiation has acquired an adversarial component. People have come to approach negotiation with the idea of "winning."

Mediation—When people need some help, they bring in a mediator to facilitate their conversations. The agreement is voluntary; the mediator does not make decisions!

Resolution—Although similar to mediation in that agreements are voluntary, resolution differs because the resolutionary takes more responsibility for getting to resolution. The resolutionary is committed to more than the process; the resolutionary is committed to a resolution that allows people to get on with their lives. The expanded definition of resolution that is found at the beginning of Chapter 21 guides the actions of a resolutionary. Getting to resolution might incorporate any of the options within the continuum.

Neutral evaluation—In neutral evaluation an expert evaluates the situation and makes an advisory recommendation.

Mini-trial—A mini-trial is similar to neutral evaluation. A mock jury makes an advisory decision that you look to for guidance.

Arbitration—Arbitration is an adversarial proceeding in which the law provides the standards for how issues are decided. It's like a trial, except more informal than civil court proceedings. It can be binding or only advisory.

Trials—Trials are a formal adversary court proceeding—a "civilized" mode of war. Formal rules of evidence determine what the "decider" takes into consideration.

Remember, you have the power to design a process, and you can creatively combine options to provide the best process for your situation. This was expressed very clearly by Dean Karl Llewellen of the Columbia Law School in the 1930 classic *The Bramble Bush*, a primer for incoming law students:

> This doing of something about disputes, this doing of it reasonably, is the business of law. And the people who have the doing in charge, whether they be judges or sheriffs or clerks or jailers or lawyers, are officials of the law. What these officials do about disputes is, to my mind, the law itself.[31]

What the people involved decide, based on the standards they think are important, governs the situation. How a particular situation is resolved is *the law* for that particular situation!

Advocacy and Adversarial: Knowing the Difference

Having looked at the broader perspective, let's look at some concerns about today's reality. I remember my introduction to "the adversary system." When you probe and listen to the underlying concerns of the other side, accommodation and satisfaction for everyone is possible. Solutions could be invented to accommodate the interests of both sides. Sometimes, strong partisan advocating for each side is the best way to understand all of the parameters of a situation. You must, however, know the important difference between advocating strongly and being adversarial. Many people operating today ignore the difference.

You can advocate a position when you know that the other parties are honorable, although they are championing a different position. It is essential to realize that effective resolution comes from relationships created by an honorable attitude. Unfortunately, over the past few years, "Rambo" tactics have become commonplace. Things were becoming so out of hand that a Chicago judge issued a report about incivility with recommendations that included rules to guide attorneys' conduct. The prescribed conduct under the new rules reads like "manners you forgot to learn from your parents."

When you choose an advocate, be mindful of the distinction between advocacy and adversarial, the costs listed in Chapter 2, and the suggestions for selecting a professional in Chapter 25. Make sure you choose an effective advocate, someone creative enough to design the best process for your situation.

Sometimes the Courthouse

In certain situations, formal legal procedure and judicial adjudication is the only way to resolution. You must know when that is the best alternative. Some indications are:

1. When one or more parties will not voluntarily engage in constructive efforts to resolve the matter: for example, a partner takes control of the books of a business, an insurance carrier refuses to make payment, or one party in a divorce refuses to make any kind of payment unless ordered by the court.

2. When one party wants to set a precedent for the future: for example, a manufacturer that is being sued for punitive damages may want to clear its name to prevent future extortion.

3. When public officials can only take action based on judicial authority: this can happen because of uncertainty that needs

legal interpretation, legislative requirement, or the political expediency of shifting responsibility.

4. When you have legal rights you want to enforce.

Some Thoughts About Our Current System

The existence of the teeth of the formal legal system that is always present in the background is part of what enables the process of resolution to work. This became clear to me a few years ago when I was talking to a colleague who had taken on the task of bringing conflict resolution skills to the former Soviet Union. His task was formidable. For many years citizens had lived in the paradigm that there was no such thing as conflict. People had little experience of personally engaging in dialogue to get to resolution. They always received answers from a higher authority.

The relationship between the absolute control of the former Soviet Union, freedom, and anarchy is a very curious edge. Even though I personally don't like conflict and recognize that litigation is a form of war, I know that we need a place that will provide fairness for anyone abused—by government, a business, or another individual. Our current systems and safeguards provide that place. Given the increasingly complex transactional milieu we inhabit, however, it is time to examine that process. The foundational principles of the system were designed hundreds of years ago. It is time to revisit some of its premises. Even though the system functions, it is subject to the abuses that arise from the people that play major roles—lawyers, litigants, judges, and juries.

We need a system that helps makes democracy work! Otherwise, we will have the "chaos" of anarchy or the "chaos" of absolute control. The fail-safe of our system provides a remedy against abuse every day—irresponsible manufacturers, abusive governmental action, and irresponsible individuals. But it is time to see if we can do better. This book provides some suggestions.

Summary

What separates us from a state of anarchy are the safeguards of a legal system in the background that people can access when they have been abused by another. Before resorting to that system, there is a continuum of less invasive processes available that work because of the legal system in the background.

Reflections

Think about some of the conflicts you are currently facing. Given the choices mentioned in this chapter, what do you think the best options are? Why?

Chapter Twenty-Five

Choosing a Professional: The Resolutionary

One cool judgment is worth a thousand hasty counsels.

—*Woodrow Wilson*

The person you choose as your guide is critical to the kind of resolution you will get. Whether you're alienated from your partner of 15 years, fighting an antitrust battle with the Justice Department, or dissolving a two-year marriage, the style of your advisor is critical.

If you choose a professional to resolve a conflict, make sure you create a partnership and clearly define your desired outcome. Use the agreement process in Chapter 20 to build a joint vision! The process will serve you well. It will help you to choose the right person.

As I mentioned in Chapter 1, contextual research for this book consisted of interviewing about 100 senior conflict resolution professionals I call *resolutionaries*. Who are resolutionaries? These professionals know that their brand of resolution creates lifetime clients. I am fascinated with the way resolutionaries discern real concerns.

They know how to honor and respect what is presented, and how to find a vessel that holds everyone's concerns.

Their tradition accommodates and balances competing concerns. Black or white, right or wrong, or win or lose is not the point of their inquiry. They understand effective resolution. Their core message: Fighting is a waste of precious resources—energy, time, money, emotions, and property. They understand that after every war, the political settlement then addresses the issues. Escalating conflict avoids addressing what really needs attention.

In this chapter I want to share with you more fully what resolutionaries do and how to recognize them, so you can select them in an informed way and know what kind of relationship you should expect to have with them.

What Resolutionaries Do

Resolution is the healing of conflict. The process of resolution provides a safe environment in which healing can take place. When disagreement is present, a resolutionary engages in the following kind of analysis:

1. Who has what concerns in the situation? What is each party's "reality" about the situation?

2. How quickly must action be taken? What's the measurable loss and continuing risk of nonresolution?

3. Who is needed for effective resolution?

4. How do we get everyone to the table in the right mood? Who needs attitude adjustment, and what's the best way to do it?

5. What constraints exist?

6. Are there any laws, regulations, principles, customs, agreements, or other standards for the situation?

7. What future relationships are essential?

8. Are there other special concerns?

9. What is the best action plan? Who will do what, when?

In selecting a resolutionary, I suggest observing the candidate's analytical approach and comparing it to the one above.

Competencies of a Resolutionary

The following list explains the competencies of a resolutionary. Please use it as criteria for selecting a professional or for evaluating one you have already chosen.

Collaborative: A resolutionary enjoys the engagement of working with you toward resolution. Resolutionaries treat you respectfully, are authentic, and learn well with others.

Common sense: A resolutionary makes the complex seem simple.

Confident: Resolutionaries are clear about the value they contribute. They are not afraid to act on their assessments.

Creative and innovative: Resolutionaries invent what they have to do to get the job done.

Empathy: Resolutionaries feel for you and your situation, and they honor and legitimize your concerns.

Fairness/not winning: Resolutionaries understand that tomorrow is another day and that each day is a victory when you are treated fairly.

Faith and trust: The resolutionary knows that every situation can be resolved no matter how bleak it may look. That faith resolves many impossible situations.

Generating openness: In resolving conflict, it is essential to have the disagreement in the open. Resolutionaries provide the presence that lets you open up and talk about what happened and your emotions. They create an environment of trust that opens the door to resolution.

Getting to the core: Resolutionaries have the uncanny ability to see through to the core of the conflict. They know what must happen to get to the bottom.

Honesty and integrity: Trust is at the core of a resolutionary, and you trust resolutionaries because you believe they will effectively advocate your concerns and the concerns of everyone else.

Intelligence: Resolutionaries are very smart. They "know" what's happening.

Judgment: Resolutionaries have been down the road many times. They know the territory. They have a sixth sense about what will work and what won't.

Life experience: Resolutionaries are often bald, or gray, or possess an old soul. They have mileage on them.

Listening skills: Resolutionaries understand what is being said and know what's behind the words, and they know what's not being said. They know each person must be heard, and they know how to do it. They listen with their eyes and with their entire body.

Maintaining control of the process: Resolutionaries watch the process mindfully because once the process gets out of hand, there is no hope of an efficient resolution.

Open-minded: Resolutionaries don't have a vested interest in a particular resolution. They keep the ball in play and let the resolution discover itself.

Practicality: Resolutionaries are practical. They do not let personalities or principles stand in the way of sound decisions. They understand what forums are best for working out different kinds of issues.

Taking care of people: Resolutionaries know that at the core of all disagreements there is a people-related issue that must be resolved. When you take care of the human concern, the "problem" often takes care of itself.

Tolerance for conflict: Resolutionaries remain fair and centered even though the situation is highly charged.

The remainder of the chapter will discuss key aspects you should expect in your relationship with a resolutionary.

No Hourly Billing

The key to success and partnership in most law firms is your annual number of billable hours. Do you think that impacts professionalism? Resolutionaries know that there is an inherent conflict of interest in hourly billing—resolving the conflict as efficiently as possible versus the self-interest of the attorney, either to make partner or to earn more. One wise advisor I know charges a fixed fee, or he tells clients that he does not know what the cost will be but promises that they will not be unhappy about the fee—and they never are. My suggestion—agree on a fixed fee.

For intrapersonal conflict, we turn to therapists. They also charge by the hour, and that process of resolution can turn into a lengthy, expensive process. Unfortunately, no one provides firm promises about outcomes.

Supporting Clients

Resolutionaries support clients in taking personal responsibility. They know that only involved individuals can go to the core of the breakdown in relationships. When you abdicate responsibility, it is difficult to identify and resolve the conflict. This is where most lawyers get sidetracked as they shift the focus to the "legal" issues. By focusing on legal principles and legal issues, effective resolution becomes impossible; the areas that require you to be the most engaged and vulnerable are not addressed.

The core competence of resolutionaries is their ability to lead you to a new vision that returns you to the real business of your life. They support clients' personal growth by keeping the focus on the most vulnerable concerns and talking about them intelligently. Resolutionaries operate from the principle that their job is to lead you to resume collaboration with more effectiveness. Their responsibility is providing lubrication that gets you back to productivity.

When you develop the habit of more effective communication and collaboration during the resolution process, the pathway you built for the resolution will continue to serve you in the future. This reflects what Professor Robert Baruch Bush calls the *transformative aspect* of conflict resolution.[32] Building these pathways makes the "legal" issues easy to resolve.

Resolutionaries have a higher calling—upholding principles embodied in the Ten Commandments. They know these are the laws on which civilized society rests. (Attorneys are part of that tradition, though many young lawyers have little contact with it.) Resolutionaries can rekindle that connection. They often provide elegant outcomes. Their master-strokes are often *su wen* in character. (*Su wen* describes a single-needle acupuncture treatment so masterful that it catalyzes a sequence of events that cures the difficulty and returns the system to functional harmony and equilibrium.) The solutions of the resolutionary reestablish the working relationships that are essential for business, family, or governmental activity. They provide options that contribute to the present and future quality of your life.

Partnering in Producing Resolution

Clients often do not know what their trusted advisors do for them. Resolutionaries make sure you know what they do before they do it, and why it must be done. They form partnerships with you for producing results. The relationship is the opposite of your going to be "fixed." The resolutionary seeks to preserve your resources by letting you do as much as possible.

Consequently, resolutionaries often serve as process designers. The process chosen is essential in determining the outcome. For example, if you have stomach pains and consult a surgeon, you may end up with surgery. A nutritionist, internist, or massage practitioner will provide a different intervention in the same circumstance. Resolutionaries are not locked into a single path or perspective.

Trust

The importance of *trust* cannot be overstated. The integrity of the resolutionary is the catalyst that brings the situation to a head. Because of the high level of trust, agreement can result from the resolutionary's sharing an advisory opinion about what he or she thinks is a fair resolution. I have seen these recommendations resolve multibillion dollar claims.

Years ago, to support his application to practice law before the courts of another state, my friend Al needed the recommendation of a judge he regularly appeared before. He was pleasantly surprised when he read the recommendation. It said that contrary to most of the lawyers who regularly appeared before him, the judge was always impressed with Al's candor. He could always be counted on to tell the truth. Al was surprised that others would act any differently.

Expect this level of trust from a resolutionary!

Creativity

Resolutionaries use their creativity to get the job done. They do whatever it takes. They are not limited by what they think is right or wrong. They often design from outside the boxes in which most people think. I know a resolutionary who serves as a coach and guide for people who are going into court by themselves without counsel. Another resolutionary acts as a consultant, without anyone knowing he or she is behind the scenes. Whatever role they play, it is always purposeful and chosen consciously.

Resolution does not face some of the formal constraints of traditional processes. It is an arena that has no boundaries. Nor is it for the fainthearted. To make that same point my colleague Jeffrey Kichaven recently wrote an article called *Mediation Is Not for Sissies*.[33] I agree. When there is no "right" way and you start exploring the emotional relationship issues, you don't know where the process will lead. You must trust your creativity to design the next appropriate step.

Serving the Situaton

Resolutionaries know that the key to what they do lies in serving the needs of the situation. In one situation, a resolutionary was placed on the horns of a dilemma about personal income, client service, and the honor of a promise. He was entrusted with the custody of a document that contained essential information about an ongoing dispute. He was representing the interests of his primary client, a client who was responsible for half of his income.

His client assumed that the resolutionary would turn over the information to him because of their relationship and because no one else would know. The resolutionary refused. His client told him that he would be taking his business elsewhere if the disclosure was not made. The resolutionary still refused. That night he hardly slept, tossing and turning all night. He had one young child and was expecting another; the loss of this client would put his family in immediate financial jeopardy. In the midst of his turmoil, just after he became absolutely certain that his honor was more important than anything, the phone rang. It was his client, calling to apologize for the untoward demand.

The resolutionary thanked his client and shared his concerns: if he disclosed the information, he would lose both his honor and his client. Once it was demonstrated that he was not totally honorable, how could his client trust that the resolutionary would not sell him out? The matter was resolved to everyone's satisfaction the next day, and he gained a client for life.

A Resolutionary Is Not About Being Nice

Bryan was terminating a long-term relationship with Gene, his business partner. The situation had a number of financial, contractual, personal, and emotional facets. On his lawyer's advice, Gene would not communicate with Bryan. A meeting was arranged. Because Gene was being unreasonable, the mood was tense. Bryan thought Gene had no intention of resolving the difficulties between them.

Gene and his attorney mirrored the mood of unreasonableness. The attorney was doing a better job of being a jerk than Gene was. It was as though the attorney had some unfinished business to work out with the world, and Bryan's number had come up. On top of that, there was a long business association between the attorney and Bryan's partner; the attorney had acted as counsel for the partnership during its two-year existence.

I had a sense of a potential resolution before any conversation with Bryan, his partner, or his partner's attorney. The meeting was arranged to resolve the various issues, but many concerns needed addressing. Would a relationship continue? Would it take a new form? If a major contract was secured or if the company was sold to an investor, what would Bryan get? Everyone wanted to explore the old deal and also look at several speculative new ideas.

After hellos I said, "We are here to resolve this today!"

I was crisp, clear, firm in setting the mood and checking to see if there was hope that resolution was possible given the animosity. Because of other people's unreasonableness and personal insults, I became agitated and started pacing. I was bothered to the point that I had to restate the intent of the meeting. I wanted to make sure that it was absolutely clear to everyone, and also to focus the conversation. I was there to resolve the matter, that day. Meanwhile, Bryan saw no possibility of an early resolution, and he was getting uncomfortable because of all the hostility. The attacks continued. The room heated up. The pitch increased. Tempers were getting closer to their edges—most of them; not mine.

As the boiling point neared, my instinct and focus sharpened. The more unbearably hot the room became, the more settled, calm, cool, purposeful, and agile I became. I was angry, but firmly and deliberately I kept my voice icy, fierce: "If you say one more nasty comment, one more cruel word toward this man you will regret it. Stop it! Now!"

Bryan had never seen me look or sound like the man who was now his advocate. I was laserlike, clear as crystal, assertive as a radar lock, dangerous, almost lethal. But not out of control, not abusive, not unkind, not uncompassionate. Every cell in my body was aligned. They were all pointing down this attorney's throat. He got the message! Suddenly, he was mute, inanimate.

The mood instantly shifted. In the quiet you could feel the resolution begin to speak its voice. Even in the silence, you could feel the resolution in your chest, coming to the surface. Reaching agreement about the business matters became a simple matter. The mood and intention that I set helped make that possible.

To do this work effectively, resolutionaries must hold a safe space that allows others to be OK, no matter what is on their mind. They must have the patience to allow each side to say what needs to be said, from whatever the source. I warn my clients about this, so that they do not feel alone in the resolution process. But I am accountable for holding the intention of resolution, and that requires holding a context that is large enough to encompass all parts of the situation.

The knowledge of that necessity informs every instinct of my being. Whatever must be done, will be done. Don't make the mistake of thinking that the way of the heart is always nice and sweet or that elegant conflict resolution is always pretty. A resolutionary can be lethal. Sometimes you have no choice.

Summary

When choosing someone to help you resolve a conflict that you have tried but can't resolve yourself, make sure you select someone who will partner with you, not someone who will do it for you. Look for someone who listens, has independent opinions, will set a fixed fee, talks about the human aspect of the situation, and doesn't take him- or herself too seriously. The role model of the resolutionary provides a standard to be followed.

Reflections

What qualities are most important for the professional who helps you? Take the time to write them down. Do you know anyone who fits the bill? Describe them. Then, for 21 days—the time it takes to "install" a new habit—pretend you are a resolutionary.

Life is too short to be little.

—*Disraeli*

Part VI

The Power
of Resolution

*Now that you understand how the
conflict resolution model works,
Part VI projects what your life will be like
when you adopt and master the principles
and practices of resolution.*

Chapter Twenty-Six

Practicing Resolution in Your Everyday Life

We look forward to the time when the Power of Love will replace the Love of Power. Then will our world know the blessings of Peace.

—*Gladstone*

Tuesday

It's Tuesday morning. You just woke up after a fitful night. Just before you fell asleep, Matthew, your husband of 9 years, broke the news that the company he has been with for 8 years finally offered him the job he has been pining for—responsibility for implementing a new companywide employee development program. He told you that he accepted on the spot, even though the position will require immediate relocation from San Francisco to Cleveland. You politely offer congratulations, but your reaction is mixed. You are happy for him, but you don't know how you can support the move, given the impact on your career and on your 14- and 15-year-old daughters from a prior marriage. You are also angry because he did not consult with you before making the decision.

The situation is complicated further because you have just been made a partner in the group medical practice that you have been with for six years, and you recently promised your kids that they can complete high school in San Francisco. At the moment you don't know what to do. Keeping to yourself, you quietly dress and head off to your office.

At your office you find that you have just been put in charge of the team of nurses and staff that support other professionals with various specialties. Your office manager recently attended a workshop on self-directed work teams, and he wants to implement that concept in the practice. You have to work with him because you are on both the management and finance committees. Recently, staff members have been grousing because they want more control over their work. So forget the notion that you get to give orders because you're the boss who provides a salary. Those days are gone.

Around noon the administrator of the HMO that sends you 35% of your business calls to tell you that it is in the process of signing an agreement with a local hospital that may result in your losing all or a portion of that business. You just want to go back to bed! There are two phone messages waiting when you return from lunch. One from your mother, and one from the secretary of the Board of Education, of which you are the president. Your mother is upset because your father is insisting on moving to Arizona, and your board is being threatened by a teachers' strike. Things just got worse. Mercury must be in retrograde. You begin to wonder what the afternoon will bring.

You have your hands full, but you are not worried as you observe the strong emotional reactions you have to all of these potential disasters. You have faith that you will get through these crises with little *Sturm und Drang*. You are confident that all of these conflicts will have great outcomes for everyone concerned. You remind yourself that an attitude of resolution will best serve you. Since you have so much on your plate, it's critical to remain focused and not waste emotional energy.

After some reflection you sit down and make a prioritized list of what needs attention and the action you will take.

1. Call the HMO, find out why it is changing hospitals, and schedule a meeting.

2. Call the Board of Education and schedule an emergency meeting with the president of the teacher's union.

3. Call your mom and dad, tell them you'll see them Saturday for lunch and get their situation resolved then.

4. Call Matthew and tell him you (a) love him and are very proud of him, (b) want to take him out to dinner on Saturday night, just the two of you, and (c) that you need to speak with him about your concerns over his promotion and how it will impact the family.

5. Call Roberto, your office manager, and schedule a meeting to discuss the idea of reorganizing the support staff.

As you check off the list, you feel proud of your ability to move into a state of resourcefulness. You acknowledge how fortunate you feel to have a roadmap to take you through these situations to a place of resolution.

You quickly call the executive director of the HMO and request a meeting for 6:00 that evening, after you have finished with your last patient. You tell him that his HMO is your most valued client, that you will do what you must to keep its business, and that you want to see him to learn about why the HMO is considering another provider. You are pleasantly surprised at how receptive he is to meeting with you. You acknowledge to yourself how valuable the attitude of resolution is.

You decide to call the president of the teacher's union yourself. The first thing you say when she takes the call is that you want to meet with her to resolve the outstanding issues in the contract negotiation. You understand that she is sensitive to the effect on the community of children, parents, teachers, and all of the lives that will be impacted by a strike. You tell her that the teachers must be very concerned over the current status of their contract if they are considering a strike, and it is your intention to listen to the concerns and reach an agreement. She acknowledges your contacting her directly, your willingness to quickly move beyond posturing, and the sincerity of your message. You feel that you're picking up momentum as you agree to meet Wednesday at 5:00 PM and keep going as required.

You call and find your mother in a hysterical state of high drama. The thought of moving away from her children, grandchildren, friends, and the house she has lived in for 40 years is making her crazy. Even more disconcerting, your father won't discuss it. His mind is made up, and that's it. You tell her that you will call him and that you promise to get it resolved over lunch on Saturday. She calms down a bit. You call your father and tell him he is being inconsiderate by making such a big decision unilaterally (as your husband did). You ask him to have lunch with you and your mother. You ask him to come to lunch with an open mind. He agrees to apologize for not consulting your mother and to come to lunch and keep an open mind, but he says he is still moving. You say, "Thanks, I'll see you Saturday."

You get your husband on the phone. You tell him you love him, and that your relationship will survive whatever career choices need to be made. You tell him that even though you know how important the promotion is to him, you were upset by how inconsiderate he was in not discussing that with you. It flies in the face of all the covenants your marriage is based on. You ask him to have dinner with you Saturday night, at his restaurant of choice, so you can fully discuss and quickly resolve the situation. He accepts. You sense he is holding onto his "male career prerogative," so you know the conversation will not be a simple one. You assure him again that you want to support him and understand how important the position is to him.

You call your office manager and set up a meeting with him for the next morning at 7:30 AM.

You take a deep breath and reflect on how good you feel. Even though the situations are challenging, you have taken a proactive posture with all of them. The balls are in play, and even though the discussions won't be easy, they are already moving forward. You feel good as you start your afternoon schedule of patients.

On your way over to the HMO, you start thinking about the history of the relationship between your medical practice and the

HMO. You can't understand the reasons for its change of heart. You decide that your objective for the meeting is to leave with the basis for a new agreement, and that the most important thing you want to find out is the conditions of satisfaction for a successful ongoing relationship.

You exchange pleasant greetings with Dan Johnson, and then you get right to the point. You ask Dan what's going on. He says that the changes have nothing to do with any performance problems on your part, that the situation is a result of a corporate acquisition of their company. Their new parent has an agreement with the parent of the local hospital. He tells you that nothing is written in stone, and the primary concern remains the best possible treatment for their patients. You tell him that it is important to you not to lose any of their business and that you will do what is necessary to maintain their business and the relationship. You want to craft an agreement that will make explicit the "partnership" that has been implicit. Most important, you want the information that will enable your organization to be their ideal provider.

He says OK. You proceed to work through all the elements of the agreement template that you have learned. You discuss a vision for patient service, the promises each of you must deliver on to enable that level of service, how you will measure satisfaction, concerns each of you has, and a specific method for resolving conflict. You thank him for his participation and that you will put the understandings into a written form for each of you to reference. As you are about to leave, he says "Thank you. I have never felt so thoroughly listened to about what we want from our independent providers. If we can live up to the agreement we have just crafted, we will be functioning within a partnership few believe is possible." You say thank you and remind him that this is only the first step.

That night your husband is especially attentive. He wants to talk about the move and your feelings. You give him a kiss and say that you think it is a good idea to hold off on the discussion until dinner Saturday—that the notion of each of you having some time for reflection will do you both some good.

Wednesday

The next morning you meet with your office manager, Roberto, at 7:30. He is very excited about constituting the entire office support staff of 22 as a self-directed work team. You ask him what that is. He says that it is an organizational form in which the team members set goals, performance standards, schedules, compensation, and evaluation criteria. You tell him that to you that means they will run the show in terms of their work.

Given some of your recent managerial reading about increasing productivity, you like the idea. An article you read reported that most workers perform far below their capacity because they have little respect for the people managing them and for how the managers evaluate them. The article's ideas made sense to you. You see self-directed work teams as a step in the right direction. You give the idea your blessings. You also request that Roberto set up the process in which an agreement between the "team" and the practice is put in place, as well as agreements between each individual and both their team and the practice. It has been your aim to get everyone to express his or her individual needs and to get the full benefit of what each individual can give to the practice. You see the team concept as a great way to implement an open environment—developing each person to be fully responsible for what he or she does. You tell Bob how pleased you are with the new structure that will be put in place. You make yourself available to support the process in whatever way you can.

Going into the meeting with the president of the teachers' union has you filled with anxiety, because of the potential impact of a strike. You ask her if the meeting can be "off the record," as you want to have a very frank conversation. You tell her that you have recently learned about a process designed to bring every element of the conflict out in the open, and you ask if she will participate. She agrees, on the condition that in each step you lead the way. You say "yes" and off you go. You have already stated your intention to do your best to resolve the situation. You emphasize how essential authenticity is to get the outcome you both desire.

You each tell your respective stories about the current situation. Then you serve as both guide and participant in a completion process. What is quickly uncovered is that on the prior advice of counsel, each of you has been posturing and withholding critical information. Their advice, though sound within the traditional legal paradigm, has promoted a game of brinksmanship. The conversations let you step into the shoes of the union president. Now that you have a complete picture of the situation, you see a potential resolution. You propose a solution. She accepts. An agreement in principle is reached, to be implemented by your attorneys. Given your success, you ask if she wants to meet next week to work on an "agreement for results" that could create real partnership between the teachers and the administration.

You feel fulfilled as you pull into your driveway. After the completion process with the teachers' union president, you turned into collaborators looking for the solution that would take care of everyone's concerns. The requests of the teachers were seen as legitimate, as were yours. You became creative designers, looking together at the big picture you both had a stake in resolving. Tomorrow is another day, but so far you are three for three!

Thursday and Friday

You move through the rest of the week with a sense of elation. You are beginning to trust the notion that conflicts provide an opportunity for the highest expression of yourself. Being conflict-adverse, as most of us are, you never realized that working through to resolution could enhance and affirm your life so much. You are so pleased you made the choice to learn a systematic way to get to the other side.

When you hit the pillow on Friday, you have a better sense of who you are as you reflect on the way you have handled the week's challenges. You sleep soundly, once again resisting your husband's attempt to talk about his promotion.

Saturday

After your morning hospital rounds, you arrive for the pow-wow with Mom and Dad. It amazes you that after 40 years of marriage, your parents don't have a clue about how to engage in a productive conversation in which real communication takes place. They are still living in a world of fault, blame, being right, and withdrawal. One divorce and a number of difficult relationships have forced you to examine the arena of human interaction. You realize that every generation has new horizons to explore.

You ask Mom to tell her story. Then you turn to Dad. You have to sit on both of them to prevent interruptions and editorial comments. You ask them what has worked about the marriage, and they lighten up as they recall a lifetime of wonderful memories. They loosen up even more. You ask about what doesn't work, and you hear the kind of things that are bound to arise between two human beings who have shared over 40 years. When you ask them to forgive each other and themselves, they do so. When you ask them to thank each other and God for bringing them together, they do so. When you ask about what else needs to be said, they both say that they don't care where they live, as long as they are together. They each take responsibility for being inconsiderate and obstinate.

You can see the resolution forming. You turn to them and ask if either has a proposal. Dad says that he will give up his plans to move, that it is not worth the guilt and aggravation. Mom says OK, but she wants him to have as much Arizona as he needs. They agree to spend a fourth of their time in Arizona, and the rest in San Francisco. Now you can have a swim, and catch up on some paperwork at your office before dinner with Matthew.

As the cooling texture of water runs over your body, you start to think about your conversation with your husband. Deep inside, you are nervous and feeling very vulnerable. You don't really know where this is going. The marriage will change. At worst it may end. Watching Mom and Dad in action provided some inspiration in terms of the value of longevity in a relationship. As you move into a flipturn and push hard off the wall, the messages of all your teachers provide healthy guidance:

1. A key to life is knowing that all we can do in any situation is:

   Be present in the moment.

   "Listen"—externally and internally.

   Speak what is true for you.

   Do not be attached to particular outcomes.

2. The most vulnerable and most important place in the continuum towards resolution lies in "not knowing" the answer. Our ability to stay in that place until clarity arrives is the key to uncovering the best outcome.

3. The best framework for any difficult situation is to "learn" our way through it.

Now you feel prepared!

You return home and dress for dinner. You and Matthew head to his favorite restaurant. Despite the difficulty of the situation, you feel more beautiful and alive than you have ever felt. You are ready for the conversation.

After ordering, you open the conversation. Since you know the resolution process, you orient him to the structure of the conversation and the attitude of resolution you would like them to adopt. You tell him that you will be looking for a creative resolution that will take care of both of you. Because of your clarity and the mood of resolution that you have established, he agrees to participate fully. You take a deep breath and start to tell your "story."

You tell him how much you care for him, how important your marriage is, and how much you value what you have built. You tell him how much respect you have for his achievements and how you don't want to stand in the way of his advancement. You tell him that you want to see everyone in the situation satisfied. You tell him that you can't leave San Francisco, but that you won't stand in his way. You feel lighter as the words pour out of your heart. He tells you about his anguish over the juncture you have reached—his fear and his desire. He feels that he must choose between you and his career, and it is a choice he does not want to make. He knows there is no right or wrong in the situation, that the only way to get to the bottom is to respect each other. He understands your concerns, but it seems clear to him that his whole life, all that he has worked for, is tied up in this moment of destiny.

You both feel suspended in a womblike cocoon as you continue the birthing process of finding resolution. Your dialogue is like Michelangelo chiseling away at the excess to uncover his master-pieces. As you begin the completion process, your energy starts to flow. You delineate what works in your marriage—the foundation and oasis it provides; the good company; intellectual stimulation; ro-mance; minimal amount of friction; economic partnership; raising the children; respect; autonomy; vacations; love; the fact that it functions when so many marriages are falling apart. There are things that don't work: career demands of time, focus, and energy; Matthew's some-times acting the way he thinks a man should act, like his acceptance of the position without discussion; your ex-husband's impact on your kids; career orientation of both of you; your fear and vulnerability. This is not as difficult as you thought it would be.

You are in agreement about what you have to be thankful for: that you found each other after both of you had unsuccessful marriages; your home, children, family and friends; your respective careers; the grounding foundation your marriage provides. Identifying whom you each have to forgive is very instructive for both of you. You forgive Matthew for being overly protective of the girls and for the times he doesn't honor your career needs as he honors his own; his sometimes excessive flirtations; his broken promises around household mainte-nance; his being overly critical of your cooking. You forgive him for his success and ambition—the drive he has demonstrated has pro-vided a healthy income and put you through medical school, but it has also resulted in the current cross-road. Matthew forgives you for your school-board activities; your refusal to join him in skiing trips; your messy home office, and your cats. Most of all he forgives you for your successful career and the devotion you have to your parents, children, and the community.

As you forgive each other for the positive attributes of your separate lives, a mood of respect and admiration begins to emerge. You see each other in a more profound way. An element of admiration and support for the concerns and aspirations of the other starts to surface. You each experience the grief that change brings. You both feel the sadness of disappointed expectation of what you thought your life would continue to be. You feel some fear about the changes and of day-to-day separation. But the resolution seems clear to both of you.

To be complete, you each needed to say that you were committed to making the transition, the separation, and the marriage work.

It was agreed that Matthew would move to Cleveland, set up housekeeping, and return at least every other weekend. You left all the other details to be worked out later. One thing that was agreed was that you were partners for life; nothing would get in the way of that. The rest of the evening was deeply intimate, a closeness you will never forget. When you reviewed the conversation and your feelings about it, you had a sense of well-being beyond any you ever felt. You knew in the deepest part of yourself that this man was your mate and that you were just taking off on another great adventure together. You started to see all the opportunities present in the new era—the era you named "Separation, Growth, Autonomy, and Adulthood."

Year End

At the end of the year you reflected on the value of the attitude of resolution, and your growing mastery with the resolution process. You and Matthew are both thriving. The marriage could not be healthier. Although the transition was not simple, instead of often being frustrated and torn by the conflict of other priorities, you seem to be spending more quality time together. Each of you is freer to devote full attention to the vocation and causes you are committed to. And when you come together, it's like a honeymoon.

Matthew is being considered for a division presidency. You have been made a full partner in your practice. The agreement you put in place with the HMO was so well received they are sending you more patients than you have time for. So, you added two more physicians to your staff. Your office staff has increased its productivity by 33%, and the mood around the office is one of teamship and support. Your agreement with the teacher's union was hailed as an innovative model—both the procedure and the substance. You have been appointed to the State Board of Education and have been traveling around the state teaching others how you did it. Your parents' establishment in an Arizona retirement home has added a level of zest to their marriage—they couldn't be healthier or happier.

As you get ready to ring in the new year, you feel grateful for the lack of conflict in your life. You are producing results way beyond expectation—and having a great time. You kiss your napping husband and roll over to let the warmth of the sun caress your face.

A man receives only what he is ready to receive. . . . We hear and apprehend only what we already half know. . . . Every man thus tracks himself through life, in all his hearing and reading and observation and travelling. His observations make a chain. The phenomenon or fact that cannot in any wise be linked with the rest of what he has observed, he does not observe.

By and by we may be ready to receive what we cannot receive now.

—Henry David Thoreau

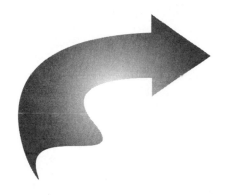

Endnotes

[1]A client who had a flair for promotion coined this phrase as I guided him through a series of sensitive negotiations.

[2]The statistic was cited in the following article, by David Hoffman, "How To Keep Your Company Out of Court—New Methods of Dispute Resolution," *Directorship*, Vol. 22, No. 2, February 1996 (Greenwich, 1996).

[3]Interview with Alvin Toffler, *Wired Magazine,* November 1993.

[4]The story about BQ is found in Joel Barker, *Paradigms: The Business of Discovering the Future* (New York, Harper Business, 1993).

[5]Jerry B. Harvey, *The Abilene Paradox and Other Meditations on Management* (New York, Lexington Books, 1988).

[6]Steven Covey, *Seven Habits of Highly Effective People* (New York, Simon & Schuster, 1989).

[7]Roger Dawson, *Secrets of Power Negotiating* (Hawthorne, NJ, Career Press, 1995).

[8]Angelis Arrien, *The Four Fold Way* (New York, HarperCollins, 1993).

[9]John Kabat-Zinn, *Wherever You Go, There You Are* (New York, Hyperion, 1994).

[10]Margaret Wheatley, *Leadership and the New Science* (San Francisco, Berrett-Koehler 1992).

[11]Robert Benjamin, "The Mediator as Trickster," *Family Mediation Quarterly*, Vol. 13 (San Francisco, Jossey-Bass, Fall 1995).

[12]Edward DeBono, *Conflicts, A Better Way to Resolve Them* (London, Harrap Limited, 1985).

[13]The term *Open Book Management* appears in Jack Stack, *The Great Game of Business* (New York, Doubleday, 1992).

[14]Rachel Naomi Remen, M.D., *Kitchen Table Wisdom* (New York, Riverhead Books, 1996).

[15]Scott Peck, M.D., *The Road Less Traveled* (New York, Simon & Schuster, 1978).

[16]Bill Lamond, a trainer and consultant, first introduced me to a form of "The Completion Process."

[17]Robert M. Bramson, *Coping With Difficult People* (New York, Anchor-Doubleday, 1981).

[18]Max DePree, *Leadership Is an Art* (New York, Doubleday, 1989).

[19]Deepak Chopra, M.D., *Creating Affluence* (San Rafael, CA, New World Library, 1993).

[20]Napoleon Hill, *Think and Grow Rich* (New York, Fawcett Crest, [rev. ed.], 1960).

[21]Maxwell Maltz, M.D., *Psycho-Cybernetics* (New York, Simon & Schuster, 1960).

[22]The STI Group (Steuart Place, San Francisco, CA) developed a model of leadership called "Extending Your Power and Influence."

[23]James Kouzes and Barry Posner, *The Leadership Challenge* (San Francisco, Jossey-Bass, 1987).

[24]Max DePree, *Leadership Jazz* (New York, Currency Doubleday, 1992).

[25]Humberto Maturana, *The Tree of Knowledge* (Boston, Shambhala, 1992).

[26]Matt Ridley, *The Origins of Virtue* (New York, Viking-Penguin, 1997).

[27]Dr. Steven Covey, *Principle Centered Leadership* (New York, Summit, 1991).

[28]Tom Petzinger, the *Wall Street Journal* (New York, February 25, 1997).

[29]The principle of self-organization is also the premise of Margaret Wheatley and Myron Kellner-Rogers, *A Simpler Way* (San Francisco, Berrett-Koehler, 1996).

[30]Dr. Fernando Flores called these areas "Domains of Permanent Concern."

[31]Karl Llewellen, *The Bramble Bush* (New York, Oceana, 1930).

[32]Robert A. Baruch Bush and Joseph P. Folger, *The Promise of Mediation* (San Francisco, Jossey-Bass, 1994).

[33]Jeffrey G. Kichaven, *Mediation Is Not for Sissies* (*Los Angeles County Bar Association Litigation Newsletter*, Vol.13, No. 2, Winter, 1996).

Selected Bibliography

Aburdine, Patricia and Naisbitt, John. *Megatrends for Women* (New York, Villard, 1992).

Acland, Andrew Floyer. *A Sudden Outbreak of Common Sense* (London, Hutchinson Business, 1990).

Arrien, Angelis. *The Four Fold Way* (New York, Harper Collins, 1993).

Bandler, Richard. *Using Your Brain—For a Change* (Moab, Utah, Real People Press, 1985).

Bandler, Richard and Grinder, John. *Frogs into PRINCES* (Moab, Utah, Real People Press, 1979).

Barker, Joel. *Paradigms: The Business of Discovering the Future* (New York, HarperBusiness, 1993).

Bush, Robert A. Baruch and Folger, Joseph P. *The Promise of Mediation* (San Francisco, Jossey-Bass, 1994).

Champy, James. *Reengineering Management* (New York, Harper Business, 1995).

Chopra, Deepak, M.D. *Creating Affluence* (San Rafael, New World Library, 1993).

Coelho, Paul. *The Alchemist* (New York, Harper San Francisco, 1993).

Covey, Steven. *Principle Centered Leadership* (New York, Summit, 1991).

Covey, Steven. *Seven Habits of Highly Effective People* (New York, Simon & Schuster, 1989).

Crumm, Tom. *The Magic of Conflict* (New York, Simon & Shuster, 1987).

Dana, Daniel. *Talk It Out* (Human Resources Development Press, 1990).

Dass, Ram and Gorman, Paul. *How Can I Help: Stories and Reflections on Service* (New York, Alfred A. Knopf, 1987).

Dawson, Roger. *Secrets of Power Negotiating* (Hawthorne, NJ, Career Press, 1995).

DeBono, Edward. *Conflicts, A Better Way to Resolve Them* (London, Harrap Limited, 1985).

DeBono, Edward. *Serious Creativity* (New York, HarperBusiness, 1992).

DePree, Max. *Leadership Is an Art* (New York, Doubleday, 1989).

DePree, Max. *Leadership Jazz* (New York, Doubleday, 1992).

Dyer, Dr. Wayne. *Gifts from Eykis* (New York, Simon & Schuster, 1983).

Edelman, Joel. *The Tao of Negotiation* (New York, HarperBusiness, 1993).

Eisler, Riane. *The Chalice & The Blade* (San Francisco, Harper & Row, 1987).

Fisher, Roger and Brown, Scott. *Getting Together* (Boston, Houghton Mifflin, 1988).

Fisher, Roger and Ury, William. *Getting to Yes* (Boston, Houghton Mifflin, 1981).

Fritz, Robert. *Creating What You Always Wanted To* (Salem, Massachusetts, DMA, 1985).

Goleman, Daniel. *Emotional Intelligence* (New York, Bantam, 1995).

Hanh, Thich Nhat. *Being Peace* (Paralaax Press, 1987); *Touching Peace* (Paralaax Press, 1992); and *Peace Is Every Step* (Bantam, 1991).

Henry, James F. and Lieberman, Jethro K. *The Manager's Guide to Resolving Legal Disputes* (New York, Harper & Row, 1985).

Hill, Napolean. *Think and Grow Rich* (New York, Fawcett-Crest, 1937).

Katzenbach, John R. and Smith, Douglas K. *The Wisdom of Teams* (Cambridge, Harvard Business School Press, 1993).

Keen, Sam. *Fire in the Belly: On Being a Man* (New York, Bantam, 1991).

Knebel, Fletcher and Clay, Gerald S. *Before You Sue: How to Get Justice Without Going to Court* (New York, William Morrow, 1987).

Kolb, Deborah M. (Ed.). *When Talk Works* (San Francisco, Jossey-Bass, 1994).

Kouzes, James M. and Posner, Barry Z. *The Leadership Challenge* (San Francisco, Jossey-Bass, 1987).

Kouzes, James and Posner, Barry. *Credibility* (San Francisco, Jossey-Bass, 1993).

Maltz, Maxwell, M.D., *Psycho-Cybernetics* (New York, Simon & Schuster, 1960).

Maturana, Humberto. *The Tree of Knowledge* (Boston, Shambhala, 1992).

Mindell, Arnold. *The Leader as Martial Artist* (San Francisco, HarperCollins, 1992).

Moore, Thomas. *Care of the Soul* (New York, HarperCollins, 1992).

Morgen, Sharon Drew. *Selling with Integrity* (SanFrancisco, Berrett-Koehler, 1997).

Moss, Richard, M.D. *The Black Butterfly: An Invitation to Radical Aliveness* (Berkeley, Celestial Arts, 1986).

Moss, Richard, M.D. *The I That Is We* (Berkeley, Celestial Arts, 1981).

Naisbitt, John. *Megatrends* (New York, Warner, 1982).

Naisbitt, John and Aburdine, Patricia. *Megatrends 2000* (New York, William Morrow, 1990).

Notarius, Clifford. *We Can Work It Out* (New York, Putnam, 1993).

Peck, M. Scott, M.D. *The Road Less Traveled* (New York, Simon & Schuster, 1978).

Peters, Thomas J. *Thriving on Chaos* (New York, Alfred A. Knopf, 1987).

Peters, Thomas J. and Waterman, Robert H., Jr. *In Search of Excellence* (New York, Harper & Row, 1982).

Peters, Tom. *Liberation Management: Necessary Disorganization for the Nanosecond Nineties* (New York, Ballantine, 1992).

Quinn, Daniel. *Ishmael* (New York, Bantam/Turner, 1993).

Rand, Ayn. *Atlas Shrugged* (New York, Random House, 1957).

Rand, Ayn. *The Fountainhead* (New York, Bobbs-Merrill, 1943).

Reid, Alan. *Seeing Law Differently: Views from a Spiritual Path* (Ontario, Canada, Borderland, 1992).

Remen, Rachel Naomi, M.D. *Kitchen Table Wisdom* (New York, Riverhead Books, 1996).

Ridley, Matt. *The Origins of Virtue* (New York, Viking-Penguin, 1997).

Robbins, Anthony. *Unlimited Power* (New York, Fawcett Columbine, 1986).

Rogers, Carl R., Ph.D. *On Becoming a Person: A Therapist's View of Psychotherapy* (Boston, Houghton Mifflin, 1961).

Saint-Exupéry, Antoine de. *The Little Prince* (New York, Harcourt Brace Jovanovich, 1941).

Senge, Peter. *The Fifth Discipline* (New York, Doubleday/ Currency, 1990).

Stack, Jack. *The Great Game of Business* (New York, Doubleday, 1992).

Toffler, Alvin. *Powershift: Knowledge, Wealth and Violence at the Edge of the 21st Century* (New York, Bantam, 1990).

Ury, William. *Getting Past No* (New York, Bantam, 1991).

Vail, Peter B. *Learning as a Way of Being* (San Francisco, Jossey-Bass, 1996).

Weeks, Dudley. *The Eight Essential Steps to Conflict Resolution* (New York, Putnam, 1994).

Weisbord, Marvin R. (Ed.). *Discovering Common Ground* (San Francisco, Berrett-Koehler, 1992).

Weisbord, Marvin R. and Janoff, Sandra. *Future Search: An Action Guide to Finding Common Ground in Organizations and Communities* (San Francisco, Berrett-Koehler, 1995).

Wheatley, Margaret. *Leadership and the New Science* (San Francisco, Berrett-Koehler, 1992).

Wheatley, Margaret. *A Simpler Way* (San Francisco, Berrett-Koehler, 1996).

Williams, Margery. *The Velveteen Rabbit or How Toys Become Real* (New York, Doubleday, 1922).

Wilson, Larry. *Changing the Game: The New Way to Sell* (New York, Fireside, 1987).

Wylie, Peter. *Can This Partnership Be Saved?* (Upstart Publishing, 1993).

Zambucka, Kristin. *The Keepers of Earth* (Honolulu, Harrane, 1984).

Zambucka, Kristin. *The Mana Keepers* (Honolulu, Green Glass, 1990).

Index

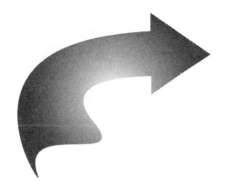

About the Author

Stewart Levine is the founder of RESOLUTIONWORKS. His personal mission is to change the way our culture currently resolves conflicts: To become reliant on resolution and agreement for its business and personal relationships. *Getting to Resolution* is drawn from 25 years of experience as a lawyer, manager, consultant, mediator, and trainer.

Levine began his career advising and representing public officials as a Deputy Attorney General for the State of New Jersey. He practiced law actively for ten years, representing individuals and corporations in civil and criminal trials; and overseeing complex commercial and real estate transactions. While working on his Master of Laws degree, he taught at Temple University Law School, where he was a Law and Humanities Fellow.

Levine was a panelist for the San Francisco Bar Association Symposium on the Future of the Legal Profession. He holds a human resources appointment from the Law Practice Management Section of the American Bar Association. He has written a number of articles advocating resolution as the highest art of legal service. The ideas in Levine's articles were endorsed by the House Judiciary Committee in its examination of case resolution in the Federal courts. These ideas appear as part of the *Congressional Record*.

In six years at AT&T, Levine was recognized as a pioneer "intrapreneur." He taught empowerment and *intra*preneurial business development seminars to managers as the company moved through divestiture. He was a partner in charge of business development for a consulting company that moved from servicing the small business market to working with Fortune 500 companies.

Levine combines a dynamic blend of powerful insight and creativity. He has been recognized for his skill in creating agreement and empowerment under the most challenging circumstances. He uses his approach to help form teams and joint ventures in a variety of situations. Companies he has worked with include American Express; Caterpillar Corporation; Chevron; ConAgra; Crosby, Heafey, Roach, & May; Deloitte & Touche; EDS; General Motors; Herman Miller Corp.; Oracle; Safeco Insurance Company; the U. S. Departments of Agriculture and the Army; and Visa USA. He also works with small companies, partnerships, individuals, and couples.

Levine has trained companies in the United States, Australia, Canada, England, New Zealand, Ireland, and Scotland. He teaches classes on management, self-directed work teams, collaboration, communication, conflict resolution, and business writing. He has spoken before a broad range of audiences including the Commonwealth Club of San Francisco, the American Bar Association, the U. S. Attorney's office, the Bowie State University Forum on Conflict in the Workplace, the Syracuse University Entrepreneurial Forum, and the Phil Donahue Show. His writing has appeared in many professional journals.

Levine graduated from the Maxwell School of Economics at Syracuse University. He is an honors graduate of Rutgers Law School where he was Student Writing Editor of the *Law Review*. He lives and works on Alameda, a beautiful island in the San Francisco Bay.

RESOLUTIONWORKS

Reading a book can be very helpful for resolving conflict. I hope *Getting to Resolution* has been useful for you.

This book shares the wisdom of many teachers, and stories of resolutions I have been part of. I invite you to participate in a continuing dialogue about "getting to resolution." If something in this book troubled, touched, helped, or inspired you, please write and tell me. I am very interested in hearing about effective resolutions, the widespread use of resolutionary thinking, and the resolution model. Please share your creative ideas and stories so I can share them with others.

You can help spread "resolution" with products and programs offered by RESOLUTIONWORKS, a training and consulting firm committed to helping individuals and organizations experience the peace and power of resolution.

RESOLUTIONWORKS offers:

- Speeches and custom meeting presentations
- Audiotapes and videotapes
- Conflict resolution services for business and personal matters
- Workshops for organizations committed to creating cultures of resolution and agreement

If you wish to share stories, or want more information about speeches, workshops or materials, please contact:

RESOLUTIONWORKS
(510) 814-1010
Fax (510) 814-1010
E-mail: ResolutionWorks@msn.com